Traitor to India

Also by Sasthi Brata

My God Died Young
Confessions of an Indian Woman Eater
She and He

Traitor to India

A SEARCH FOR HOME

Sasthi Brata

 Paul Elek   London

For P___
H___ and S___
the three who bore the brunt of my ego

First published in Great Britain 1976 by

Elek Books Limited
54-58 Caledonian Road, London N1 9RN

Copyright © Sasthi Brata 1976

ISBN 0 236 40039 8

Printed in Great Britain by Biddles Limited, Guildford

Contents

		Page
Part One		
1	Whispers of Immortality	10
2	The Trial	30
Part Two		
3	The Condemned Playground	54
4	Journey into Carnage	78
Part Three		
5	Retchings of a Soured Cynic	98
6	The Collector	109
7	Decline and Ascension	123
Epilogue		156

Author's Note

I should especially like to thank Peter Preston, the present Editor of the *Guardian,* for publishing two long journalistic pieces which I have drawn upon in this book. For the rest, during the time of writing, several extracts have appeared in the *New Statesman,* the *Hindusthan Standard, The Statesman* (India) and the *Illustrated Weekly of India* — my sincere thanks to the Editors of these publications.

I have purloined, either intact or in part, most of my chapter titles from more eminent wordsmiths. Thankful acknowledgments to the following: Thomas Stearns Eliot, Franz Kafka, Cyril Connolly, Reinhold Nebuhr, John Fowles and Edward Gibbon.

While *The Waste Land* was being composed, under the original title of *He Do The Police In Different Voices,* Heisenberg had stumbled upon the theory of Matrices, which ultimately led to the formulation of 'The Principle of Uncertainty'. I divined that the temporal conjunction of these two mighty phenomena, contrasted with their spatial and disciplinary disjunctions, must be of some profound, though as yet unperceived, significance. I therefore attempted, presumptuously perhaps, to exemplify dissonance, ventriloquism and harmonious resolution, in the third and final part of this book.

The interface between Reality and Illusion, the transitional no-man's-land between fact and invention, has been the obsessive hunting ground for saints, novelists and poets all the way from Aquinas and Dostoevsky down to Hesse, Caudwell and myself. In exact literal terms nuclear physics and mystical philosophy meet here.

In this book I have tried to conduct a conversation with myself, sealed within a literary acoustic structure, in the hope that it would echo and resonate in more than a personally restrictive dimension. The criteria of success are of course the ambitious ones of reverberations effected without intention, reflections produced in mirrors one cannot see. To achieve my objectives I have allowed imagination to cannibalize the sacred and inviolable body of 'objective truth'; I have aided and abetted Fancy in ravishing the maidenhood of 'documentary reportage'. I have also perpetrated a few other canonical misdemeanours, but to adumbrate further would be both impertinent and impolite. So, to borrow a phrase, I shall withdraw and ring up the curtain.

S. B.
London

Truth is a qualificaton which applies to Appearance alone. Reality is just itself, and it is nonsense to ask whether it be true or false. Truth is the conformation of Appearance to Reality. Thus Truth is a generic quality with a variety of degrees and modes. In the Law Courts, the wrong species of Truth may amount to perjury. For example, a portrait may be so faithful as to deceive the eye. Its very truthfulness then amounts to deception. A reflexion in a mirror is at once a truthful appearance and a deceptive appearance. The smile of a hypocrite is deceptive, and that of a philanthropist may be truthful. But both of them were truly smiling.

Alfred North Whitehead

If I had turned to other pursuits I should have put my soul in danger. I began to write, not to display my learning — which is nothing — but to reveal true facts lying hidden in ancient confusion.

William of Malmesbury

PART ONE

1

Whispers of Immortality

A man who has been the indisputable
favourite of his mother keeps for life the
feeling of a conqueror, that confidence
of success that often induces real
success.

SIGMUND FREUD

When her husband died two years earlier, she had said to her eldest
son, 'You shouldn't have taken away the Master, you shouldn't
have burnt him. He was only sleeping, poor man. You have made
a grave mistake.' Her voice had been low and brooding, as if she
were talking to herself. No hysteric sobs had followed. Quietly, she
had set about performing the rituals required of a newly-widowed
Brahmin woman. And it was then that they had known she had lost
her mind.

Now some two years later those same faces that had been gathered
round her husband's death-bed were looking on at her. And they all
believed that she was about to rejoin her Master in a well-earned
Heaven — the moment of departure was imminent. Her second son
was incantating verses from the *Gita* in Sanskrit, in the belief that
such reverent sounds would assist her soul's flight to the higher
reaches of the other world. Her eldest grandson held a spoonful of
holy Ganges water poised over her parted lips, occasionally letting a
drop slide down her tongue. And the only daughter held her feet
between folded palms in a gesture of the last homage to mother. The
others in the room were all part of her immediate family. And they
moved about noiselessly on bare feet, spoke in whispers, afraid to
puncture the sacramental shroud that surrounds a departing soul.

The wooden venetian blinds were drawn to keep out a burning sun.
Tubes of light, speckled with dust, streaked in through the cracks.
Cobwebs nestled in corners of the ceiling, the grey-green marble
topped table heaved under the weight of numerous phials and
medical concoctions. The dense dark air in the room carried the
odour of decaying flesh, and incessant incontinence had injected the
acrid smell of ammonia. The bed clothes, which bore stains of night

soil, added yet another viscous aroma. Breathing was hard here, movement slow; life was being squeezed out.

The doctor had said, 'No hope at all,' the day before but no one was quite certain when the end might come. There had been a threesome vigil all night long and now at mid-morning there were drooping eyes and stretched nerves all round. Ears perked to sharp attention each time there was the faintest sound of discordant breathing. While the glazed eyes blinked signs of life with the transparent stare of unrecognition. The invisible pall-bearers had arrived but they were taking their time to lift up the load.

The woman on the floor who was the focus of all this attention was seventy-two years old. Her face was fleshless, a membrane of parched skin stretched tight over bone. In her present horizontal position, she measured four foot seven inches from head to toe. Over the years she had shrunk in size. The arched vertebrae, bowed legs and even the neck which refused to hold her tiny head aloft, had all conspired to show the weight of age bearing down upon her. But she was not a tall lady at the best of times. On her fortieth birthday, a few months before her youngest son was born, the attending nurse had pronounced that she was 'less than five foot in height'.

But out of that frail and diminutive frame had issued fourteen offspring. Ten of them had died at ages ranging between ten days and two years. Only four had survived till now. And apart from the wives, everyone who was looking on at her now was the loin-fruit of those surviving issues — progenies, progenies of progenies, and yet again. Her great-grandson, who frivolously skipped round the room in one of his mother's rare moments of unleashed carelessness, was only two years old. But there was one face missing amongst her onlookers — her youngest son, who was away in England.

And in all that Hindu assemblage, it was the missing face which arched towards biblical allegory. For her youngest son was the prodigal, the black sheep in the family who had forsaken the parental home and stoked his mother's heart with the aches of separation for ten long years. Yet now on her death-bed, if she had words to speak, she would have wanted him by her side, touched his brow once more and whispered a last blessing before the final silence sealed her lips. Those who stood round her were always there, dutiful, unchanging. The absent son was the missing piece, and had he arrived in time, before she drew her last breath, perhaps her eyes might have shed the scales of senile indifference, flashed one last time with the bright glow of unremitting love.

But the test wasn't made and the look on the face of the dying woman held an earnest plea to the very end. For if her past life had flashed across her psychic screen in the final moment, there would have been few frames of fulfilment and happiness. Pain had been her constant life-long charge and one by one the fuses had burnt out, till she no longer bore the burden of feeling. Memory of the immediate past was the first to go, then the faculty of recognition. Some six months earlier she had asked her daughter who she was. When that happened, the loving mother she used to be and the shrunken lump of unresponding flesh she had now become were separated by an unbridgeable gulf. It was the daughter who now felt the pain and the legacy had passed on to the next generation.

The story of that legacy began a year before the turn of the century. She was born in a village in East Bengal (now Bangladesh), the daughter of a local school-teacher. The family were high caste Brahmins but poor. Her mother died when she was one year old and her father remarried — this time the aunt, her mother's sister, 'to keep it in the family'. Her step-mother began producing a brood of children — some eight of them — almost immediately after marriage. So her earliest childhood was spent in the company of relatives and neighbours. By the time she was six, and old enough to help with the housework, she had learnt the signal lesson she would never be allowed to forget for the rest of her life — rely on no one but yourself. What little schooling she had came from her father, when he could spare an evening. And her fondest memories of those childhood years pivoted round the rare occasions when she would sit on her father's lap and hear him read aloud the story of Rama and Sita from the epic *Ramayana*.

When she was just over thirteen, her marriage was arranged with a 'very propitious family' — *zamindars* (petty landowners) from a neighbouring village. The groom-to-be was a handsome young man of thirty who had graduated in Civil Engineering in 1905. He was the first in his clan to enter the portals of European education and take up the 'menial' role of 'employee' in the big bustling metropolis of Calcutta. There had been mixed feelings about this but it was generally agreed that such things as Engineering and Western clothes, though inferior to Sanskrit learning and Brahmin punditry, were indices of 'progress'.

The would-be bride and groom did not set eyes on each other till the day of their marriage, but consummation must have taken place very soon after the wedding. For the husband left his wife in the village to go back to his job in the city and the small girl produced her first child in less than a year, before she was fifteen. The birth was difficult, the baby boy screamed incessantly for two whole days after his entry into the world. The midwife confessed that 'this was a most unusual case'. But as there were no doctors in the village, treatment was confined to offering *puja* to the Gods in the morning and sprinkling holy water the rest of the time. Despite these efforts however, on the tenth day after its birth, the infant died.

The elders in the family decided that there was no call to inform the father about the mishap as he was not due any leave from his job till the next year. And of course there was no question of his coming away on unpaid leave of absence — after all, he was the sole prop to the family finances. If he was to be told it would unnecessarily upset him, when there was precious little he could do about it anyway.

The child-mother desperately longed to tell him of their mutual bereavement, to share her sorrow with the Master. But since she could not write herself, she had to seek help. And no literate member of the household was willing to put her words on paper. So she continued to send her husband sheets of drawings — in envelopes on which he had written down his own address — which tried to express her feelings. And each time he interpreted those sketches to mean that their child was alive and well, though he did reflect that his baby son must be something of a horror in appearance for his mother to portray him in that way. From the rest of the family who did write to him, there was no hint that his son was no more. Nearly a year later, when he came home to the village for the annual festivities, he learnt that his first born had died — and not very recently either. He decided then, against strong family pressure, to take his wife back with him to Calcutta, the city in which he worked and lived for most of the year.

The wound in the mother's heart was not healed but she felt the stirrings of hope and love for the first time.

The two of them set up house in a small room in one of the shabbier parts of the city, as most of his wages were sent off to the folks back in the village. The furniture consisted of a narrow bed, a table and two chairs. All their clothes, the few pieces of jewellery she had been given by her father and sundry other possessions, were housed in a medium-sized tin trunk which was pushed up against one corner of the room. In the tiny verandah next door, she did the cooking on a portable coal cooker, washed her clothes and occasionally doused herself from head to toe. It served as bathroom, kitchen, laundry-base and dining area — they would sit cross-legged on the floor and eat with their hands off brass dishes. The lavatory, little more than a hole in the ground, was two storeys down on the ground floor.

It wasn't much of a home but she was mistress here, away from the prying, domineering eyes of her elders. She was proud to be living in the big city (none of her sisters-in-law had ever visited Calcutta), married to a man who mixed with 'white sahibs' and wore trousers to work every morning. She called him 'the Master' because a wife was forbidden to mouth her husband's name and Master seemed an apropriate label for this strong, handsome man. He mostly referred to her as 'the woman', though he did sometimes send a chill down her adolescent spine by calling her 'the Mistress'. If this wasn't perfect bliss, it was the nearest she had come to happiness so far in her short life.

For the first six months after their arrival in Calcutta, the two of them at least enjoyed the privacy and pleasure of their own company. The man did not believe in talking very much, least of all about feelings. He was her husband, she was his wife; the roles were strictly defined, there was no need to investigate nuances. Indeed it is doubtful if it occurred to him that there were any. He would be a good spouse to her and she would be expected to return the compliment. Outside this small area of marital life, there was the wider terrain of devotion and loyalty to 'the Family', reverence for elders and adherence to the book of Brahminic rules. He was moderately well versed in Sanskrit, socially he was impressively gracious, and in his profession he was something of a pioneer. So he would work hard and make money, look after his kith and kin, perform the morning *pujas* and keep his wife warm in bed. Sufficient unto its duties was his life thereof.

He was a patient teacher, she was a responsive pupil. In a short time she had learnt to read and write Bengali. This spurred him on to higher goals, he bought her a copy of *The Primary English Reader*. But that project was doomed from the start as she held the firm belief, instilled into her by her father, that women who learn English — 'the foreign poison' — become widowed early in life. Other than in this one instance of insubordination however, she was an ideal housewife. She washed and mended his clothes, scrubbed the room clean every morning, cooked homely vegetable dishes and kept a tight rein over the housekeeping money — she even managed to save a few *annas* every month out of her meagre allowance. Her needs were small and they were met. She could not call herself discontented.

Then, expectedly, the course of their lives changed. She conceived for the second time and her husband sent for female relatives in the village to come and look after his teenage wife (she was not yet seventeen) during the last few months of pregnancy. The twosome life of husband and wife was over; the young woman's hegemony over that small room came to an end.

The first influx consisted of two older sisters-in-law. And the three women slept on the floor while the man of the house occupied the only bed in the room. Of course the housework continued to be done by the juniormost member of the female trio. But now she had the benefit of being instructed and advised by her seniors.

The young girl resented the intrusion. But since she and her husband were never alone, there was no way of telling him what she felt. Besides, she was not too sure that her feelings were not a tiny bit unholy. 'Never question your Master's decisions', her father had said the day before she was married. And it was the Master who had decided to bring these women into their house. So she nursed the infant in her womb and the pain in her heart in the same solitary body, dreaming of the day when the wise elders would return to the village, leaving her alone with her husband and her child.

But the Master had different plans for the future. He had great faith in himself and was determined to do good for humanity — especially for his kith and kin. And as he had been given a rise in his job, he could afford to spread his largesse over a wider field. He believed you should not work for yourself alone. If Fate had smiled upon you, then it was your duty to help those who were needy and less fortunate. So he rented an extra room and sent off invitations to some younger members of the family to come and join him in the city: 'There are greater opportunities here, you could make a life for yourself.'

Of course the invitations were accepted and the villagers poured in. But since they were Brahmins, they could not do menial jobs. And as none of them was qualified in any sphere, and as 'the right type of work' was hard to find, the burden of providing for his unemployed relatives fell on the engineer who wore Western clothes to work every morning.

This was a turn of events which the Master had not anticipated. He had fought his way up in the world, worked his passage through school, college and engineering institution, on scholarships, tuitions and odd jobs. He had never turned his nose up at any work which brought in money. But his relatives were not disposed to bestir themselves. They had been invited to Calcutta by the successful city man. So it was up to him to provide sustenance, jobs and anything else they might require. This was the traditional Hindu ideal of hospitality and they would have nothing less than the ideal from their man in Calcutta.

Perhaps it was pride which prevented the Master from asking these idle relatives to pack their bags and go back home to the village, where they could at least feed on rice and potatoes grown on their tiny plots of land. Perhaps it was the challenge. Perhaps even, he really believed in the Hindu 'ideal' of hospitality and refused to admit having fallen short. Whatever his reasons, he did not share them with his wife. But he did expect her to share his burden.

Just as he started working sixteen-hour days, so he wanted her to do the same. There were some fifteen people living with them (they had an extra room by now, three in all), and she cooked, washed up, charred and laundered for the entire household. On top of this she did some sewing to earn those crucial extra *annas*. Frequently she did without a meal.

And all the while the infant in her womb continued to grow.

Though she would have preferred an easier plight, she did not feel there was any choice. She accepted the role of an unpaid over-worked domestic as a fact of life. At times she even allowed herself to covet a crown of virtue. The Master treated the world as a challenge — she was willing to be his handmaiden in this heroic dual. It was enough that she was his wife; there was no other prize she longed for. At least not at this stage of her life.

So if she was underfed and ill-clothed and if her pregnant condition induced fainting fatigue, it was the will of God — who was she to complain? And when the boy was born prematurely, a lump of ill-formed flesh weighing less than four pounds, she blamed no one. She felt fear and prayed to the Gods that the infant might survive. And in fact her prayers were answered. Or so she thought. The notion of luck did not figure in her theology. From a very early age she had decided that no misfortune, however harrowing, would make her lose 'Faith'.

So when the baby did survive the first six months of his terrestrial existence, she conceived again. A girl was born in due course. Eighteen months later, when the child died for want of medical attention, the mother said, 'It was the will of God to take her away from me. I was neglecting my duties in the house.' The same fifteen people were still living in the three-roomed flat. She was still doing her duty as unpaid housekeeper and maid of all trades. The death of her child had released time in which she could attend to the guests' comforts.

From this point on a pattern was established. She would become pregnant at intervals of eighteen months or so and most of her children would die. Occasionally, as an act of clemency, one of them would be allowed to survive. Meanwhile, back at the house, the number of guests would continue to increase. The Master's fortunes would thrive but 'the woman' would never be the beneficiary. Every windfall would be swallowed up by fresh imports from the village. The housework would grow and the health of the child-producing woman would be relentlessly ravaged beyond repair.

But the Master did not lack feelings. If his wife was expecting to give birth during one of his business trips away from the city, on his return he would always ask the neighbours if the child was still alive before entering the house. When the answer was negative, he would turn round and venture on another out-of-town mission, without going in to greet his wife. He could not bear the sight of intense grief; the wailing sounds grated on his ears. His own responses remained tightly sealed within. There was no need to display emotions with uncomforting flamboyance.

The difference between 'the woman' and the Master was crucial in this respect. When a child died, she would roll about on the floor, tear at her hair, sob hysterically for hours on end. But within a week or ten days she would return to normal. The Master on the other hand showed no visible signs of mourning; he *never* referred to the death of a child. It was as if the event had not occurred. There were many who interpreted his stoicism as indifference, or even callousness. But all those deaths left their mark; he would pay a heavy price in the end.

This hit-or-miss game with death went on for twenty years and more. During that time the Master founded an engineering business in Calcutta — the first initiated by an Indian — which flourished all through the Depression and after. Great political upheavals occurred in the country but they did not impinge upon his life. He was regarded by the European community as a technical wizard and financial genius. He came to be widely respected in his profession and the appropriate Royal Societies in London heaped honours upon him. Socially, he was a pillar of eminence. The village boy from East Bengal had won the fight in the Second City of the Empire.

But despite his success and apparent westernization, the Master never became a truly urban animal. The annual *puja* holidays were always spent back at 'home', he wore *dhotis* in the house and his mode of living remained unchanged. He built a two-storeyed brick house in the village (the only one in fifty square miles), fitted it with a flushing commode, modern bathroom and coke-fired electric generator imported from England. He was more proud of that house than of his fame in the city. Many years later he confessed to his youngest son that he had always wanted to go back and spend his last years there, amidst the mango groves and rippling streams — the place where he was born was where he wanted to die.

There was an incurable nostalgia in the man and it was shared by his wife. As the years wore on, she began to grow into one of those haughty elders she had resented so much when she was young. Her early experiences did not inoculate her against the very afflictions she had suffered at the hands of others. Instead, she fitted more and more into the same mould; tradition was rigorously perpetuated. It took time of course, but those twenty years forged a personality with the ability and the will to lay down the law as it had been laid down on her. For she had never really believed that anyone had done her wrong. So there was no need to change the system. It all happened by the will of God.

At the end of those twenty years the score was three alive, nine dead. The oldest son was about to graduate as a civil engineer, like his father. The second son was ten and had been admitted into the Royal Indian Military College — an exclusive public school run by Englishmen and once the preserve of the Princes of India. The only daughter was six and looked like growing into a very pretty girl. The family was prosperous and had just moved into a Victorian house with twenty-odd rooms. The Master did not now balk at the idea of employing servants to help 'the woman' with her housework. The relatives were still there but a substantial number had been placed in the right positions, befitting their Brahmin upbringing.

'The woman' then gave birth to her thirteenth issue, a son. And it was an event of major importance for both husband and wife. For the first time, the Master showed considerable interest in his progeny. A maidservant was employed solely to look after the infant. A new house which was being built for the family in a hill resort was named after the baby boy, 'Parises' (the exact transliteration is 'Epilogue'). The Master spent all his out-of-work hours playing with his new son. Clearly, the boy had brought about a change. Or perhaps it was his new-found affluence which enabled him to look around a little. Whatever the reason, as the months went by, Parises began to occupy a significant position in the Master's life, a position which none of his other children had ever approached. The man of steel had suddenly unmasked himself to show that he too could feel human emotion.

Then, just after his second birthday, Parises caught smallpox. This time no pains were spared. All the specialists in the field were called in, the Viceroy's private doctor was flown out from Delhi. Holy men, homeopaths and *tantrik sadhus* were also invited to try their hands. But in spite of all efforts, the mission was impossible — the prognosis for smallpox in those days was a ninety-seven per cent fatality rate. Parises died. And for the first time in his life the Master burst into loud jerking sobs. He did not go to the crematorium and spoke to no one for two whole days.

At the end of that time, when he emerged from his room, his face was striped with age. He walked about with a fixed glassy stare, as if he had just come out of a long and crushing illness from which he had not yet quite recovered. His friends, relatives and even his wife were more taken aback by this sudden metamorphosis than by the death of yet another child. The Master did not share his grief with anyone but it was clear that something crucial and irreversible had happened to him.

The death of the boy did not have the same immobilizing effect on the mother. For soon after Parises died, 'the woman' conceived again — for the fourteenth time in her forty-year-old life. The family doctor warned that the birth would be difficult: her heart was weak, she was anaemic and lacked calcium. This time she herself might not survive. Specialist opinion hinted that the pregnancy should be terminated. But neither the Master nor his wife would hear of it. Nature must take its course. And if there was Death at the end of the road, so be it. Meanwhile, no human effort would be spared to serve both mother and child when the time came.

So a priest was installed in the house to perform daily *pujas* and placate the Goddess of Destruction. Gold-wrapped talismans and holy stones were hung round the neck of 'the woman'. Along with her daily quota of medicines, she began to take measured doses of sanctified water. Astrologers were called in to predict the exact date of birth. And one of them made the cruel prophecy that 'the woman' would not last another year. But this did not deter the principal characters in the drama. Preparations went on according to schedule. Good deeds were done, reverential Brahmins were invited and princely presents distributed among them. Beggars were fed, as prescribed in the book of rules. And once a month singers came to chant holy hymns and drive out evil spirits from the house.

Whatever might happen, it was going to be an auspicious birth. 'The woman' laboured for twenty-four hours and she had to be given oxygen all that time. Towards the end, when it looked as if she might die, the Master, seated on a leather chair in the room adjoining the delivery chamber, started reading versus from the *Gita* in a loud carrying voice, so she might hear holy sounds before departure. There were some fifteen women, including the midwife, standing around the bed when it actually took place; three doctors next door, and another total count of thirty odd people in the house — holy men, relatives, well-wishers and their accompanying broods of children. They all prayed that 'the woman' might live. And their prayers were answered.

A son was born. Both mother and child survived.

As if the prelude to his birth was not dramatic enough, the baby boy entered the world in a highly significant posture. Both his tiny palms were capped round his pink hairless cranium, one on top of the other. This being the gesture that holy men make on attaining salvation or *Mokhsha*, the learned Brahmins in the house pronounced definitively that 'the child will be a man of God'. 'The woman' however was pragmatically laconic in her first remark about her new-born son: 'He must live'.

And he did, with a massive injection of extra-terrestrial aid. Copper and gold talismans were hung round his neck and arms, he was incessantly sprinkled with holy water, *pujas* were performed and sacred texts endlessly intoned in the ear of the uncomprehending child. For the first six months of its life, the infant was incubated in the fervid hothouse of Brahminic ritual.

Even in her sickly condition, the mother insisted on breast-feeding her son. But the doctors ordered that she could not have him in her bed at night. So one widowed aunt took over the duties of night nurse. Every gurgle and scream was attended to, he was not allowed to remain wet in bed for more than a minute. It was clear that this fourteenth issue would not suffer from human neglect.

At first the Master took an obsessive, if theoretical, interest in his new son, as he was not very adept at handling ill-formed lumps of flesh. But later, when the lump began to acquire some small vestiges of personality, the theoretical interest was translated into practice. The toddling infant never left his father's lap whenever the Master was at home. At night his progenital rights were restored—he began to sleep in his mother's bed. And this practice continued right up to his eleventh year, when he was sent away to boarding school.

Whether or not seeds of Oedipal obsession were sown in the child due to this closeness between mother and son during those formative years remains a matter of speculation. But paternal correctives were not lacking. The boy partnered his father at bridge parties in the club, played chess with him on the odd evening and had his clothes tailored at the same British shop that the old man patronized. In the eyes of neither parent could the child do any wrong. The boy entered puberty with raspingly exalted notions about himself. Even within the permissive child-rearing mores of Bengali society, he was incorrigibly spoilt.

At this point the boy was sent off to boarding school to be groomed into a 'pukka sahib'. The institution was run by Oxbridge Englishmen and was renowned for its rigid discipline and high academic standards. The only flaw in the set-up, overlooked by the innocent father, was that the headmaster was a fire-eating evangelist in the Wesleyan mould. From the incense-burning atmosphere of Brahmin orthodoxy the eleven-year-old boy was catapulted into the hothouse of thundering Methodism. Sex, Shaw, girls and the *Gita* were all proscribed in the school. The dialectic was explosive; a virulent punch started brewing in the adolescent personality.

Back in the Victorian mansion, the household was growing in size, according to the sacrosanct traditions of Hindu families. Only the daughter, wedlocked at fourteen, left the parental abode. The two older sons remained, married to pretty young damsels selected by their parents. Dutifully, they produced offerings of grandchildren to 'the woman' at appropriate intervals. And though lenient to an extent with the third generation, the mistress of the house enforced the law on her sons and daughters-in-law as unflinchingly as her elders had done on her in the past. Though small in size, she was truly the *grande dame* — she had had a rigorous apprenticeship in the art.

But there was one member of the family to whom no rules applied. This was the youngest son, who came home twice yearly during the vacations. He slept as late as he liked (which no one else was allowed to do), ate what he wished when he wished, and generally caroused around in total disregard of the spartan code laid down by Madame. This was partly because of an irrepressible defiance the young lad had begun to develop at school. But it was largely because Madame treated her youngest son as an errant lover, loved all the more obsessively for being a bit of a rake rather than a solid law-abiding citizen.

The analogy between son and lover was more literal than literary. The mother put her son to sleep each day by stroking his back for an hour with her small doting hands. On occasions he shared her bed at night. The adolescent boy fondled his mother's breasts quite openly in public. The bathroom door was never shut; mother and son walked in and out with the casualness of a couple in the midst of a long-standing affair. The mustard-oil body massage before a bath was an infrequent but relished ritual for both partners.

The sage who pronounced, 'A man who has been the indisputable favourite of his mother keeps for life the feeling of a conqueror ...' had little to say about the effects such obsessive maternal love has on the mother herself. At this time she was in her mid-fifties; her husband had crossed seventy. There was little work in the house: the servants and daughters-in-law did all the chores, though nominally she was still mistress of the establishment. Menopause had long ago set the seal on regular child-bearing, to which she had been committed most of her life. Religious ritual came to occupy a more prominent place in her curriculum. She visited holy men and *sadhus*, donated money and organized *pujas*. But it was all done for her baby boy — now a young man of sixteen about to enter college. It was to be expected that at some stage the son would break out of Mama's tutelage, especially as he was an alert and questing youth. But no one, least of all the mother, thought the rupture would come in quite the way it did and for the specific reasons that brought it about.

Of course Papa had committed the initial inadvertent blunder in sending the boy from such a home as his to a Methodist school run by a zealous Dickensian headmaster. But Mama compounded the felony by turning up the darker side of the coin. Every time her son came home, she insisted on his doing *pujas* every morning, mumbling incomprehensible Sanskrit *mantras*, wearing gold talismans round the arm, bathing in the holy Ganges and offering prayers to the Goddess Kali at the temple. The two sets of instruction he received, both from agencies he was expected to revere, were inexorably railed on a collision course.

Mama's growing religiosity was the work of that proverbial pair of 'idle hands'. When her son was away at school, there was nothing for her to do except pay homage to saffron-robed Brahmins and wait for her darling to come home. When he did, the habits of the past few months were not easily or instantly expunged; inertia ruled. And she expected her son to join in her activities, much as lovers are said to long to share rather than to act alone.

But two were playing the game. And if inertia held sway with her, so it must have done with him. He could not forget the sermons he had heard at the school chapel every morning, bellowed out by a towering giant with Paul Robeson lungs: 'It is an evil and wicked thing to worship idols, dolls of clay and brass, made by human hands. Christ is God and there is none other.'

Thus there was conflict: two pious but deluded lieutenants of the Godhead were duelling over the young man's soul.

In the event, Hegel won the day. Neither Thesis nor Antithesis gained suzerainty. But while the Methodist headmaster merely sighed over one more lost sheep, the mother lost her most preciously beloved son.

The bonds of tenderness which had tied mother and son together were unloosed. The kisses and hugs so hungrily devoured at thirteen were rebuffed at sixteen. The cloying octopus arms of maternal love could no longer hold the prey within its grip. There was defiance, cruel and violent repulsion.

'Have you had your glass of milk, my son?' she would ask, striding into the sitting room where he was with his friends from college.

'I don't want any milk', he would shout back. 'I am not a child any more. Why don't you leave me alone? Why don't you go and say your prayers?''

She would cry, memories would be evoked, he would feel remorse for having hurt her. And then anger, the chafing rage of a trapped animal. For there was no way out of this impasse. It was neither his fault nor hers. But then why this torment, why this unendurable insistence on possessing his soul? For he did have a soul; he had at least discovered that at school. He was a man now, he had his own thoughts. But she couldn't see that, she wanted to be with him everywhere, even in the dark growing corners of his mind.

She was wholly dependent on his love. And she could not understand this sudden change, as if he had been possessed by a demon. His hurtful words, those harsh untender gestures, so alien to the boy she had once known, came from another world not of her own making. She had lost control; the old stimulus of motherly affection provoked unpredictable and volcanic eruptions. She had read no books, there was no Freud to tell her. She knew no way of stopping the slide down the hill.

The glacial descent into alienation started in his fifteenth year. He had come home one summer and mother had insisted on his doing his morning *pujas*. Methodist dogmatism and Brahmin orthodoxy came into violent collision, for he had now developed a mind.

'Why?' he had barked. 'Why should I? It's a load of superstition anyhow.'

She was petrified, never having heard him talk this way before. And fatally, she had remained silent. As the seconds ticked past her astounded face, his impatience rose, his barking queries grew louder, and the verbal lashes of discontent intensified. Till finally she squeezed out an anaemic reply which, like a drop of smelly fat, fanned the fire into a roaring conflagration.

'Because you are a Brahmin, my son,' she had said. 'Because your father and grandfather and his father before him have always done the *pujas*. You must carry on the tradition, you must pay homage to the Family Gods.'

Alas! If only there had been a grain of logic in her answer, if only she had fed his nascent intellectual appetite with a few crumbs, if only she could have met the Methodist headmaster on his own ground, crisis would have been averted. There would have been no war. For he had wanted to be on her side, he wished to be consoled, he longed to have the anguish of choice taken from him. He had defied so as to be vanquished; he had shouted at his mother so she could punish him back to docile and acquiescing love. But his challenge went unheeded. And the long strife began.

She had failed him then. And that failure would never be undone.

The young man entered college in a rebellious mood. He would have nothing to do with either his former colleagues from school or the pampered elitists from the richer Bengali homes. Instead he would seek out 'the ordinary man', turn radical and champion the cause of the underdog.

This quest for a new identity led him first to Marx, and then, less gloriously, into the arms of the Communist Party of India. He became an atheist and an exhortative 'revolutionary'. Both Methodism and Brahminism were dumped on the pyre which mother had helped to kindle. But the past took a long time to burn out. And in his heart he knew that he was wearing his new 'faith' like a talisman to ward off the evil spirits with whom he had once kept such close company.

He also learnt that gestures were as vital as beliefs in the crusade to build a new persona. So he took to doing things which were taboo, and more specifically, to acting in ways which would hurt and disturb his mother. Thus he fancied the message would get through — he was his own man now, no longer his mother's son. But all those angry stones pelted at mother fell into the warm viscous pool of maternal love without so much as causing a ripple.

If he smoked, oh well, young people do such things nowadays, mustn't judge him harshly. If he received telephone calls from girls (unheard of in the college days of her two elder sons), oh well, it is better to have it in the open than keep such sinful practices repressed in secret. Every act of adolescent defiance was explained away, absorbed. The young man did not want his back stroked any more; he was never again going to share her bed at night. He snarled at his mother when affectionate demonstrations were made in public; he dusted off her hands whenever they rested softly on his head or shoulders.

So the message did *not* get through. And mother lived a daydream, embellishing it with fond hopes for the future, regurgitating the past to pluck out a memory here, treasure a memento there. As the gulf between reality and desire widened, she withdrew into a world of metaphor where love of son began to take the place of love of God. Her own *pujas* in the morning centred more and more round her renegade son; even the Sanskrit *mantras* were liberally sprinkled with his name. What had once been an exaggerated motherly adoration was homing towards pathological obsession.

The more deprived she felt the more her stifling arms tried to tighten round her son, and the more fierce was his rejection. The ache in the jilted lover was nurtured on fantasy, till one day it would grow into a disease, fatal and malingering. She refused to face reality, for *her* reality was lonesome, it condemned her without reprieve: there was no one else to whom she could turn. Inexorably, the wedge of his desire for independence would drive him further and further away from her. Her pain would grow, her helpless lovelorn thrashings would look more and more indecent through his pitiless adolescent eyes.

This state of affairs might have continued for a long while, finally producing that modern classic 'the divided being', materially comfortable, intellectually tepid and perpetually looking back with nostalgia to the glorious days before 'the Fall'. There would have been compromise, adjustment and a measured dose of self-disgust complemented by healthy reminders of 'self-awareness' and insight. The young man had not grown up in an unhappy home; no, it was merely, merely ... what?

It was nothing so prosaic as unhappiness or poverty. Something much more imprecise and elegiac. He had been brought to the boil, or to change the metaphor, stretched very tight. And the last link in the chain snapped apart when the girl with whom he had fallen in love in his third year at college was forcibly married off by her parents to another man.

After that there was no holding him. A society which could do this could do anything — murder, mutilate, massacre. It was all cast in the same mould: mother's weird *pujas*, the headmaster's bigotry, parental indifference to the craving for individual choice. There was an authoritarian pattern here, a rigid insistence on acquiescence which the young man could no longer accept.

So he ran away from home, desecrated all family tradition by becoming a bootblack in another city, then dabbled in journalism for a year and finally took off for Europe. From this point on, one thing was unequivocally clear in his mind: wherever else HOME might be, it would never be India.

But mother did not receive the message even then. All those thousands of miles and endless oceans would not keep her son away from home. What for him was a symbolic act of severance was to her no more than another game of hide and seek — the naughty truant on a morning spree away from school. 'Of course he will come back', she would say. 'Whoever heard of a boy leaving his birthplace? He is my son, isn't he? I know him. You will see, he will come back to his Ma.'

Tenaciously she clung to her hope and her love. Photographs of the darling boy stared at her from every corner of the room. Letters were constantly despatched, and when replies became more and more infrequent, imperious telegrams and telephone calls came to take their place. But as the young man lived in penury, an itinerant bachelor seeking shelter for a night here and a week there, the summonses seldom reached him. And for months on end he remained totally oblivious of what was going on back home.

The estrangement grew with every passing year in exile. Living in a foreign land he could see the past in sharper contours. He could compare his own adolescence and college life with that of the youngsters he saw around him. Every new person he met, each fresh experience, reinforced the feeling that he had been deprived. And deprived not only by his mother and his headmaster and the particular home in which he was born. The whole society had conspired to deny him the inalienable birthright of every man — freedom. If only he could localize the germs of the disease from which he had suffered, returning to live in India would have appeared less repugnant. At least the subject would be open to argument. But increasingly the young man came to feel that the premises of Indian society ran counter to the assumptions that any civilized man would make about a viable social ethos.

But all the while son was drawing away from the remotest possibility of returning home as a repentant Prodigal, the process was sadly and insistently reversed in mother. Her faith in his loyalty and love increased with each passing year. If he had not written home for three months, it was because 'He is making preparations to come back. He means to surprise us, you will see. Any day now he will walk in through that door and shout "Hullo". That's the way he is. I know him, he is *my* son, after all. No one knows him better than I do.'

Even when the silence dragged on from three months to six and then to nine, and still there was no sign of a figure through that door and no 'Hullo' ringing in her ears, mother refused to give up hope. Stubbornly she invented another plea for his apparent disengagement: 'He must be very ill, poor boy. I must go and look after him.' Or, 'He must be working very hard. He is going to be a great man, you see. And all great men work so hard when they are young that they sometimes forget everything else.'

Of course the son did return home for short visits. In ten years he came back three times. But nothing he could do or say would convince mother that his sojourn in the West was not a transient one. On his first visit she tried to hook him up with a pretty young Brahmin girl whom she had carefully selected. But the operation was unsuccessful: he remained unrepentantly unattached, and then it was time to leave. On the second occasion she took him along to a *sadhu* who had promised — at a price — to bring him back to the 'true path'. But the occidental vaccine in his system was by now strong enough to fight off such insidious infections. On his third visit she resorted to pleas and the old weak despotisms of motherly love. And again she failed.

The pain grew. And so did the intensity of her delusions. She could not face a future without her youngest son. Separation she could bear, if only the story would have a happy ending. The gnawing agony of absence, an insistent ache born of the loss of a lover, when there is no second chance, preyed upon her every minute. Dreams of ecstatic reunion enveloped all her thoughts and insulated her from the stimulus of reality.

(When you can never again possess the one person you love and there can be none other, the pain is constant, suffocating, and drives you to hysteria. It must be something like drowning or going under gas, except it is not all over in a minute.)

When the time came to say her last goodbye, she had withdrawn so far into a world of make-believe that perhaps even her pain had been wished away.

And now in that darkened room there was impatience. It was late afternoon and the old woman was certainly taking her time. Would she pull through again perhaps, as she had done so many times before, against all earthly odds? Should they send for the doctor and see if ...? How long could one go on reading the *Gita* and pouring endless drops of holy Ganges water down those parted lips? Not that they didn't love her, of course they did. She was their mother and they had attended to her as best they could. But what must happen, must happen. You cannot fight God's will; Death comes to everyone. She had led a full life after all, had had her fair share. And now it was the end of the road, the time to say 'adieu'. Amen!

It was the daughter who first noticed that mother's eyes had opened wide and her lips were moving, as if she were trying to say something. A sudden hush descended on the whole gathering as several ears were brought close to the dying woman's face. But no sounds emerged, and those trembling lips gave no clue to the words she might wish to speak.

But just as they were all about to give up hope, mother raised her bony right hand an inch or so above the bed, as if beckoning to her eldest son. He went to her side and the tips of her fingers touched his forehead. Almost imperceptibly her lips moved once again and her eyes brightened for an instant — she had given him her last blessing. Taking the cue, they all took turns to touch her feet and seek her benedictions. And though she was too weak to repeat her gesture, her eyes seemed alive, her lips moved and each one felt sure that there was recognition in her look.

But even when everyone in the room had paid his homage, her eyes did not shut. They continued to move, pausing for an instant at each face around her and then passing on. Her lips held a question and her face strained with the last breath of energy to force a few words out of her mouth. But those precious words were never heard. She stared for a long moment at the photograph of her youngest son next to her bed and then closed her eyes.

Soon it was all over.

As if at a signal from an invisible conductor, the women began wailing in instant unison. Their freshly unstoppered grief exploded in sound and tears, rivers of brine cascading down their faces. The sluice gates had suddenly opened, and the pressing flood which had risen inch by inch in the last twenty-four hours burst into the room, drowning everything, even the mere spectacle of a most uneasy death. The women gripped and hugged each other, spoke of mother's lifelong goodness, and exchanged consoling emblems of visible sorrow. The children started screaming, more in fright than in understanding, and were ushered out of the room by sombre-faced men who were expected to contain their turbulent emotions. The whole house was plunged into rehearsed bedlam. Servants, relatives, well-wishers, all of whom were waiting for the word in adjoining chambers, poured into the room bellowing out the news of a departed soul with gutsy lungs. Mother's death was resoundingly announced.

Her earthly remains were not to be digested in an electric oven, she had insisted on that: a proper Hindi pyre with all the Brahmin trimmings, that was her wish. And so it was to be. Who would presume to question the will of mother? What she had wanted she had always got. Or so they thought. They were all too small to dare the cosmic *Karma*, what if …? Even in death she ruled. There was a strange pervasive odour of docility all round the house. However much they had resented mother and grumbled about her sententious dominance, lying there in a heap of deliquescent flesh, the old woman assumed new dimensions of perverse authority. Once upon a time they had fumed and sputtered against her rigid regime; on small forgettable occasions one or other of them had even mustered up enough courage to utter a muted cry of defiance. But now that she was dead, her presence enveloped all living consciousness, explorations of freedom were at an end. Like a snail drawing into its shell, there was relief under convention.

The priests were called, holy men assembled, her body wrapped in hand-spun cloth, white and pure as a lily. Even the bamboo bed, sprung with coir ropes, was made at home. Unlike the Pharaohs, she took no worldly possessions with her. Burning is at least final, it does not allow for storage. Memories reside of course, not the least potently for being in the oddest of crevices. Her last journey was the greatest treason for the right happening in the wrong season — for that missing face, that is.

So when she was laid on that bed, her shrunken birdlike face showing above the covers, her feet jutting out in Sicilian repost, and all those sons and holy Brahmins lifted her onto their shoulders, no one spared a thought for the youngest son who was flying out, at that very moment, all the way from England, to snatch a glimpse of mother before she was burned to ashes. But the Almighty looked round at all the machinations He had perpetrated, and behold, it was very good.

Every inch of that three-mile path from the house to the burning *ghat* on the banks of the Ganges was covered on foot. It was a hot and blistering journey; even in the late evening the mercury hovered around ninety. The sons and grandsons took turns in shouldering the dead weight of mother. They walked barefoot, grave, silent, as befitted their role. The rest of the cortège chanted holy sounds in raucous monotonic rhythms, 'Bala Hari, Hari Bol'—'Call the name of Hari [the Lord Krishna], Hari be praised'. Every few yards the priest sprinkled Ganges water and petals of sanctified flowers, ahead and aft, to keep evil spirits away. Secular pop-corn came showering down from the hands of the rest of the company to consolidate the holy foundations. No pains were spared to ensure that mother's soul would rise to heaven.

When they finally arrived at the crematorium there were exhausted looks all round, sweaty faces and sore feet yearning for rest. But the ceremony had scarcely begun, long hours of dark tableaux lay ahead. It was not yet night; the last rays of the sun striped the yellow skin of the river. The western sky was splashed in saffron, there was a small breeze, and the other fires from the other deaths leapt and danced in the dark.

Then there was a decision to be made and it was the eldest son who would make it. Ritual demanded that the body be totally immersed in the holy river this one last time and a fresh sari, appropriately sanctified, wrapped round the dead woman. But it was doubtful if the body could take such hallowed handling at this stage. Pieces of suppurating flesh had already stuck to the bed clothes when she had been lifted onto the bamboo bed; an unholy odour of decay exuded from every pore. Mother was now too fragile to be dipped into that cold water. So sprinkling would have to suffice, and the priest set about his task with generous spoonfuls of holy water to hand.

When that was done the *puja* began. And again the eldest son played his part with dutiful dignity. Then it was the turn of the other men, the crematorium attendants, to take over. They were the untouchables, the lowest of the low who would never be allowed even to kiss the feet of a live Brahmin, but who were indispensable in this final ceremony. They were tall muscular men with shiny black skins and shaven heads. They wore only the barest loin cloths around their waists, carried long iron rods in their hands and spoke only when they were spoken to by a member of the company. They took care not to pass too close, let alone touch any of the congregated Brahmins.

Two of these men came forward, lifted the bed on their shoulders and carried it to a deep ravaged hole in the ground a few yards away. Then they piled logs of wood over the hole, placed the bed across it and then heaped some more logs on top of the body. When the pyre was made, several buckets of *ghee* (clarified butter) were poured over the mound, ready to be set alight.

At this point the eldest son, holding a lighted torch in his right hand, stepped out of the group. The priest mumbled a few *mantras*, sprinkled a little holy water over the pyre, and the whole gathering burst into a chesty rendering of 'Bala Hari, Hari Bol'. Just then the torch touched mother's lips, the *ghee* shot into flame and the burning had begun.

It was a slow lingering affair. The small flame spread leisurely from log to log till finally, tall tongues of fire licked their way into the night above. The wood crackled and spat, the faces of the black men around the pyre shone with sweat as they dug their iron rods into the pile. An hour went by before the half-charred body of mother could be seen in brief glimpses. Then suddenly, one iron rod swished through the air and smashed into the skull, cracking it to bits. Some of the men in the group turned their faces away, while the eldest son, in strict accordance with the book of rules, kept his eyes fixed on the body.

The legs twitched, one small hand abruptly clutched the air as if she were still alive. The whole body twisted and squirmed, angular jerky movements at the behest of the invisible puppeteer. The closed eyes were burned brown and then into charcoal black. Flaming logs lay across her chest as fresh wood was piled on top. More *ghee* was poured and the leaping flames danced and whistled in the deepening dark. The stars hung low in the sky while the gaze of the crescent moon rippled on the surface of the holy river.

It was a long while in ending, more logs, more *ghee*, rejuvenated tongues of flame. Bit by bit the body crumbled into ash, first the flesh and then the bones, with the help of those iron rods, which smashed down, breaking them into small pieces. And there they all stood, sons, grandsons, relatives, holy men and priests, beckoned by sleep yet preserved at their posts by duty and the abiding commitment to ritual.

It was all over with the first rays of an unseen sun climbing out of the eastern sky. The logs of wood glowed with a dying fire, the last lump of unquenchable flesh was dug out of the pit and consecrated in the river. And then there was nothing left of mother—dust unto dust, ashes to ashes ... Tired eyes and sweat-stained faces watched the final flickers of flame die out in the ground. The priest pronounced his last benediction, the black glistening men withdrew into their hut, waiting for the next passenger into the nether worlds, and the sons and grandsons prostrated themselves on the ground, offering their final homage to her departed soul.

When they returned to the big house, there was a strange hush all round. Even the children sensed an emptiness — the primal energy was lost, never to be regained.

2

The Trial

Atheism is a cruel, long term business: I believe I have gone through it to the end. I see clearly, I am free from illusions, I know my real tasks ... for about ten years I have been a man who is waking up, cured of a long bitter-sweet madness, who cannot get away from it, who cannot recall his old ways without laughing and who no longer has any idea what to do with his life ...

I have renounced my vocation, but I have not unfrocked myself. I still write. What else can I do?

JEAN-PAUL SARTRE, *Words*

My mother died three days before I reached India. When I got home, the gate-keeper said, 'She's gone!' and I took the news without a flutter. Then I ran up those stone stairs, rushed into the living room and the sudden silence hit me hard. I started sobbing. The *Family* stood round me in a ring, pregnant accusing looks on their faces, while I gripped my brother's hand and tried hard to stem the flood of tears. She was gone. There was no mother to run home to any more, no bosom to cry on, no one who would give me all she had without a mite in return. The last link with the land of my birth was finally severed: I was free. What would I do with my new-found freedom? How would I find a fresh imperative — the will to go on against all odds, powered by an insistent consciousness of absolute love?

All my adult life I had never quite accepted that mother would die some day. Of course I knew she was old and old people die. But somehow in my mind she was a being apart; decay and death would never possess her. She would go on living forever, loving me, sustaining me. Whatever else might happen, she would be there, always. I didn't wish to see her, I had no need to talk and be with her. So long as she was alive, somewhere on this earth — no matter how far from me, I felt safe. I suppose in a way mother was not a person in the flesh. For me she was a concept which had never been vanquished by the rude assertions of reality.

So I had expected to find her alive. She had had many illnesses before and I *knew* she would pull through this one too. When I had rung up from London to say I would be home within a week, they had assured me it would be all right — she was ill, but she would last, at least long enough for me to see her once more. But here I was, three days too late, without even a last look of farewell to carry away with me. Yes, I cried. I don't know for what or for whom. I felt abandoned, totally alone for the first time in my life. Something of the pain she must have suffered resurrected itself in me. I wanted my mother, wanted her desperately, if only for a moment, wanted to hold her tight in my arms, just as I had done long years ago, and to cry out, 'I love you mother, I have always loved you'.

But now she had been taken from me. The dreaded 'Yama', the Lord of Death, had stolen my darling mother, and not all the *pujas* in the world would bring her ashes back to life. I remembered the priests, and the talismans, and the clinking cymbals, and the picture of Death as a cruel and unholy monster. Memories flooded in: my childhood fears of going into dark rooms alone; the rustling leaves of trees all about our house; whispers in the sinister world which crept into the sky after dusk; those shadows everywhere, hooded figures wantonly plaguing my dreams. How I would wake up bathed in sweat in the middle of a still night, fling myself on mother in bed, feel her face, arm and hair, rouse her from sleep, make her speak, so I knew she was still alive. I did not know what Death was; I had never seen a body. I knew only it was something horrible and cold after which one could not speak or see anything. And once when mother had told me that Death was just a long sleep from which you never woke up, I had wondered what was so bad in such a sleep, why mother was so apprehensive that it might happen to me.

She always wore a look of patient sorrow. Even in her smile there was a touch of sadness, something weary and forlorn. She was very lonely I think and this made her cling to me. I was her only link with the tangible: she herself seemed to have paled into a shadow, faraway, unconnected, floating on the edges of a dream. I could not but respond.

That face appeared before my mind's eye as I looked at the larger-than-life portrait on the wall — for mother was very beautiful. She was fair and frail, with dainty hands, and eyes which were drawing and tender. There was nothing harsh about her, she seemed out of place within walls of rough unplastered cement. There was that strangely pliant feel about her, the smooth skin on a soft autumnal sky. She would wander about the house silently, her voice as mellow and caressing as a velvet petal. In her lap I would be happy, as if there were nothing outside this self-contained haven. Everything she did was noiseless and serene; one felt at peace, contented with her. Often I would sit at her feet and listen to a story from the religious books. In moments of defeat her voice would sink to a whisper; when the Gods triumphed over the Devils, it would rise again, happy. Once in a while a look of pain would steal across her face but, like lightning, tear apart the sheeted dark and vanish. The old calm serenity would appear once more. This held me strangely, for in my gloomy lonesome ways I was like her. And till I was fifteen I loved her very much.

Then that love soured and I drew away. But not before I had made her pay for having loved me so much. I savaged her with the searing anger of adolescence — for hungering after my soul, all my thoughts, everything I could call my own. No use merely not to love her any more; I had to say it, scream it aloud so she could hear and be hurt. I wanted to make her bleed, and I think I succeeded. For it was not till many years later, when I fell in love myself and felt the pain of rejection, the sharp gashes in the heart which only a loved one can inflict, it was not till then that I knew what mother must have gone through. But by then it was too late, she and I were strangers, there was no chance of reparation.

Of course the very violence of my rejection embedded her deeply in my consciousness. Had I been weaned gently, had my love for her withered naturally in the autumn, those memories, those brown leaves, would have floated away, leaving me bare to receive a new spring. But I went at it with an axe while the sap was still rising, while the tree held fruit, and in cutting her off so sharply from my life, I cut myself too. Though I didn't know how: not then.

Aeons later, three days too late, I realized that I had never really got rid of her. She had always been there, somewhere inside me, letting in the dark blue winds through the cracks, breaking certainty, giving only to take away again, raising me up to a pinnacle so I could fall to dust at a pull — oh yes, I knew her power then, the total osmotic power of a womb from which I had never emerged, an eternal fable, oscillating between cyclic resurrections and recurring burials. She had been me and I her. And now that she was dead, I was somehow deformed.

For there were no axes any more, no point of origin from which I could get my co-ordinates. It was not only possible that I was empty, it could be that I was *nothing*. Until now, every gesture I had made, every word I had written, all the glorious pontifical sounds I had ever mouthed, had all been addressed to an invisible presence. I was protected, the Gods were on my side. And suddenly there was no cover on the bed; it was wet and dark, no one was answering my cries for help, and I had to dare the question 'Why?' I had to unearth the basis of myriad assumptions in one convulsive moment.

The contours of my intellectual being were abruptly blurred. My bitter disenchantment with Indian society was no longer a separate enclave in my mind but the poison fruit of that old rebellion against mother and her obsessive love. Just as every assault on the ethos of that society had been absorbed and assimilated into the body politic, so had mother responded to my adolescent thrusts of defiance. Just as every intruder had lost his separate identity in the hygroscopic air of Indian culture, so she had sought to demolish the barriers between mother and son by taking everything in, rejecting nothing. If I had revolted against the spineless acquiescence of people around me, against the supine submission to poverty, squalor and exploitation, it was because they were macroscopic models of an identical phenomenon in my own experience with the woman who had brought me into this world.

It was the passivity of Indian society which had most outraged me in my youth. Now over a decade later, having lived in the dynamic-empirical cities of the West, I began to understand the true nature of oriental passivity. There was power in absorption; you defeat the enemy by saying yes; rape is consecrated. The phallus spurts out seed and wilts away, never to regain its assertive erection — the offspring is Mother India's alone, for the male progenitor has been dispersed, like a lump of salt in a vast ocean. If docility and obsequiousness were the most offensive features of Indian life to a Western mind, they were also the principal enigmas, the sources of secret power, incomprehensible, infuriating, but never totally expunged from one's consciousness. You can fume and rant against India but not remain unaffected by her. Every area of your being is assaulted, not by force but by the vortex suction of her womb: in the end she wins. Just as mother had done, surrendering all. She had wanted to possess my soul and perhaps she succeeded.

I became dimly aware that the notion of submitting to one's *Karma* was not as totally negative as I had once thought. It was certainly in conflict with the Calvinistic ethic of forging a future solely by one's own actions; it ran counter to the Frontier spirit. Indians had never built a New World, but they had devoted centuries to shaping and reshaping an old one. They had *accepted* the impact of external forces, and then, with the inverted authority of the vanquished, persuaded the victor to don a fresh robe, speak a new language, eat a spicier food, till the final product was uniquely Indian — a society different from the one it had just supplanted, but connected to it as firmly as the new-born is to its mother, by the umbilical cord of tradition. Nothing was destroyed, but a fresh set of genes had entered the system.

The proselytizing spirit and crusading zeal so fondly proclaimed by the West as its flag of identity were not wrong, merely unnecessary, perhaps even a trifle childish. Total disconnection from the past was not only undesirable but impossible to achieve. Human endeavour, individual action, could contribute an extra parameter to the existing system, but it could never wholly negate the forces already operating within it. In this sense *Karma* was not fatalism but a reasoned commitment to causality within a vast temporal frame which transcended the physical life-span of a specific human being on this planet. Neither individually nor collectively was the future determined; no, but the options were much more limited than nineteenth-century materialism, at the zenith of occidental optimism, had ever supposed.

Not that I accepted this thesis, not yet. But I was tempted to question the alternatives more closely. The certainty of youth, the unambiguous rejection of old-world values, the shrieking confidence with which I had once asserted, 'I shall build a new life for myself, I shall start afresh, I shall not let old prejudices hold me back' — that confidence suffered erosion. For the life I had built for myself in the past ten years was certainly different from mother's. But what of the mind, the wriggling worms of subconscious mania that infested my dreams? How new were *new* thoughts?

I had not been able to sweep myself clean of many things that mother had taught me. All the while my old friend 'Guilt' shadowed me mercilessly, and no amount of analysis would make me free of the many inhibitions I had absorbed in 'my mother's lap'.

Curiously enough, my father made a totally different kind of impact upon me. Though I remembered a time when I had been his favourite child, those memories very soon seemed distant and unreal. It was as if those events had occurred to someone else, or perhaps they had existed only in a dream.

My adolescent response to my father was not one of love or even of affection; rather, it was one of awe. From my tenth year onwards, he appeared to me as an august Victorian figure; certainly I respected him. Later, in my teens and especially after I had left home, that respect became heavily overlaid with an intense antipathy deriving from what I considered his philistinism and the way he had treated my mother.

Not even his fondest friends, I believe, would go so far as to call my father lovable. He could be gracious, witty and charming; he was certainly regnant. He never conceded to his children the right to have their own opinions. As long as there is a father, what business do sons have to think out things for themselves? Don't fathers have the best interests of the offspring at heart? And are elders, especially the pater familias, ever in the wrong? We were expected to answer this last question firmly in the negative. And we all did, dutifully, until I could stand it no more and ran away from home, causing much heartache and sorrow.

I don't mean I did the bunk because of father, no. It was the attitude he represented, the arrogance of age which I came up against everywhere I went, that sparked the fuse and shot me off into the outer space of self-discovery and self-reliance. In a way the sharp polarization of authority and subjugation he had created in our house helped me to launch out on my own. For if he had been a model liberal parent, I am sure I would not have revolted as violently as I did. My father was never a hypocrite. And that is an extraordinary achievement for a Bengali.

He did not drink or smoke, and I am quite sure he did not womanize. In my time I have done all three, in some measure, quite openly. But the backlash of guilt has never ceased to nag me. Theoretically I do not believe in the spartan life. I enjoy drinking, I love sex and my ethical values do not restrain me from any form of sensual pleasure, however bizarre it might appear to the ordinary burgher. But I do not have total control over the conditioned or instinctive responses in my being. A morning hangover or a night out with a scarlet woman finds me suffused with a suffocating sadness which owes its origins to my ascetic old man.

And since no reasons were offered for the way of life he laid down, the guilt cannot be eradicated by rational analysis. The dialectic will persist and a man divided I shall always remain. This may be considered a partial success for the part played by the father—at least the twinges of conscience remain to plague the son. I don't applaud it, nor do I feel that the endemic neurosis, sometimes verging on insanity, from which every Bengali son suffers, is a credit to the papas of the community.

The other value my father injected into me was the Calvinistic one of 'proving oneself by one's own ability — hard work, stamina and self-assurance'. And here we are on more ambiguous territory. I cannot entirely discard the validity of this doctrine, nor do I feel totally at home with it. I do know that it is a concept alien to the Indian environment — the *Gita* is specific in its instructions: 'Do *not* covet the rewards of your endeavours'. It was imported from the West and has caused a lot of misery in a lot of families. And as I suffer from it and the disease is malignant, perhaps it might deserve a little diagnostic exploration.

In my case, 'beating Daddy' is probably the most appropriate term for this affliction. I have always wanted to go one better than my father, to show myself and others that I too can get along without anyone else's help and climb high. Father told me often enough that he was a self-made man; that he had started off as a village boy and won scholarships to school and college; that he was the first Indian engineer to found a business; that he could look any Britisher in the eye, treat him as an equal and demand reciprocity. He had suffered much hardship and travail in his youth and early middle age. But by the time I was born, he was rich and well-known. And this bred an enormous conceit, a part of which I must have inherited.

There was, of course, a darker side to this shining coin. In my childhood he gave me the impression that socially he was some giant of a man. And a whole host of poor, fawning relatives sedulously fostered this notion. But when I went up to college, the disillusionment was shattering. My father was not the last word in social eminence. There were in fact a good many other fathers who were far higher up the ladder. Someone had told me a lie, I thought, and as I could not disbelieve my own experience, I put the fraud squarely on his shoulders, with just this kindness: *folie de grandeur* was my explanation of his extraordinary postures.

I now understand the reason for the discrepancy, for I have known it in my own life. As he started much lower down than any of his peers, he expected a much higher share of the applause. But of course life does not work that way. No one wants to know where you *came* from — where you've *got to* is all that counts. And it has taken me a little time to learn this signal lesson. If I have learnt it yet, that is. For it is galling to have to admit that there are some lessons which can only be learnt with age, that you cannot hurry time no matter how clever you are. Sadly, I remember how I once stabbed my father with: 'What have you done in your life?' He was over seventy then and I can still see that stricken, disbelieving face in my mind's eye as a leaden silence fell over the rest of the family.

Of course it was a typical adolescent thrust and I was selfishly and recklessly heedless of the devastation it could cause. But once those words were out of my mouth, no explanation or apology would heal the wound he must have borne right up to his death. It was no use trying to explain: I didn't mean that he hadn't done anything at all but that his achievements were not as gigantic as he would have wanted me to believe; that he had let me down by not fulfilling all the heroic conditions I demanded of my idol.

Of course to respect and admire is one thing; to love is quite another. I vividly recollect the day when, in a bus headed for downtown Manhattan, I learnt of the old man's death. The news had come in a letter from my brother-in-law which had been redirected from London. My immediate family had not bothered to contact me.

I remember feeling outrage and anger at the thought that my father had been dead for the past three weeks and I had not known about it. Then with time, as my first reactions simmered down, I wondered what difference it would have made to me if I had known at the time or even before. I felt fairly certain that I would not have flown out to Calcutta either to be at his death-bed or for the funeral. The man was over eighty-six and had been totally senile for nearly two years. During my last visit home, when I was shaving him one day, he had complimented me on my dexterity and had compared me favourably with the other barbers who attended him. Then he queried if I made a good living at the job.

I was made rudely aware that I could no longer connect him with the father I had known ten years ago. If I really loved him, I suppose fond memories might have been strong enough to obscure the senility. But since I had not even had the luck to know my father as an alert and thinking man by the time I was an adult, I could hardly, at thirty, summon up feelings of those adhesive years when I had sat on his knees.

Quite simply, I had to admit to myself heretically, my father's death meant nothing to me!

But there were a few lines in my brother-in-law's letter which gave me pause: 'Whatever we might have thought or said about him, there was never any denying that the man was a giant. With his death, an era has come to an end'.

And indeed it had. But what kind of an era? And what would follow it? Emotionally, I felt neutral. There were no tugs at the heart; no involuntary tears rolled down my cheeks; my hands did not shake. But something a good deal more insidious began to happen in the weeks that followed the day I heard of my father's death.

I began to question the basis of many assumptions I had made, *a priori* axes I had used, which had inevitably led to intellectual postulations contrary to those father had held. And as the years wore on, many of those original postulations did not seem as impregnable as they had once appeared. I wondered if, despite my obsessive and tangled love for mother, I was not really more like my father after all? Perhaps Lamarck had a point, perhaps I had not *made* myself. I was beginning to allow for the possibility that I might be the son of both my father and my mother.

Uncertainty invaded my mind at the time of my father's death just as it did two years later when I arrived in Calcutta, three days after my mother's death. But the two uncertainties were of different kinds. The first was a purely analytic variety, spurring me on towards competitive frenzy. The second made me lose my breath; it was caused less by intellectual considerations than by the absence of mother's physical body.

There were many other experiences which undermined my old certainties and seemed to slot me on a boomerang course back to the point from which I started — my mother. I had rejected Hinduism because mother had so strenuously sought to impose it upon me. I had abandoned religion, repudiated God and was determined to construct a system based on the only acceptable premises there were: Man's reason and an existential defiance of that superstitious bogeyman called 'Fate'.

Years later I had swallowed a capsule of lysergic acid and 'tripped' for sixteen hours at a garden flat in Hampstead, London. And if it didn't quite result in a Damascus-road conversion, the impact of the experience was more shattering than any other single thing that had happened to me up to that time. All the more so as I had approached the whole business with charged scepticism, treating the swelling ranks of post-pubescent 'acid freaks' with mild disdain. I had taken it to see for myself, but I was in no doubt that I would come out unscathed, my intellectual and emotional world intact.

It didn't work out that way and the small capsule produced the psychic equivalent of a violent earthquake in my being. Many, many things happened to me in those sixteen hours; I experienced a multitude of emotions and travelled in many lands, both in time and space. It brought me into collision, as no number of books or lectures could have done, with the only critical process in human life — the perception of reality.

An explosion occurred inside my head and I was transported into some timeless, spaceless land where the limitations of my physical body did not operate. To say that I felt as if I was floating would be inaccurate; rather it was a free-wheeling voyage of the mind, except that the mind had become an entity. I began to shake violently all over, as if I had been suddenly exposed to intense cold. Yet I felt warm, even peaceful. I was aware of my limbs but they seemed curiously unrelated to me. I experienced a strong sense of 'I', yet the 'I' was not the man I normally knew. This 'I' was faceless, and it was both inside me and all around me. Time was elastic, stretching and shrinking according to the whims of something beyond my control. I knew where I was, what I was doing, and yet all those movements seemed to be carried out by someone else: I perceived myself as if I were not me.

In very slow stages, an all-encompassing 'Presence' gathered round me. 'Presence' is the only way I can describe the experience, for it was neither physical nor personal. I felt that I was part of this 'Presence' and it of me. Yet in some strange way there was no division, we were a 'whole'; 'I' didn't end or begin. This 'whole' was everywhere, but it did not have a location.

In religious language I could say that this 'Presence' *spoke* to me. But in fact it was not like that at all. I became *aware*; it happened from within. There was no specific point at which anything like a 'revelation' occurred. Rather, it was as if I had known these things all along, and the covering layers of mental distraction, of physical obsession, were gently washed away, exposing what was there from the beginning. Nothing entered or left me, I simply perceived more fully.

This perception was no less real or intense than a punch in the face or a night of love. But it was not physical, neither was it cerebral. I would call it 'direct perception', where the intermediary processes of sensory stimulus, deductive or inductive reasoning, are eliminated. You just know. There is no why or how; no cause and effect. The process is totally dissimilar to anything philosophy or science has hitherto explored.

The knowledge gained from such perception is even harder to define. I knew 'I' was part of a timeless continuum which had no beginning and would have no end. And this consciousness was enough, there was no need to *do* anything about it. The 'Presence' did not urge action or prescribe remedies to social or economic ills, for in the ultimate sense these phenomena were irrelevant, they occurred to bodies and minds and things, and none of these were really 'real'. They were there all right, just as my body was right there in that very room just then. But my body was not 'me', it merely gave me houseroom, to be lived in today and vacated tomorrow. The only permanent and real thing was 'I' and 'I' was within the whole as the whole was within me.

If this 'Presence', which I acutely experienced, is to be called God, it was certainly very different from the one I had heard about at school. It laid down no law, nor was it going to dictate a code of ethics or morality.

It took a long time for the effects of the drug to wear off completely. When I finally came down from the 'trip', I was depressed, deflated and ravenously hungry. I ate a little food, drank a lot of water and fell into a deep sleep for over twelve hours. When I woke up I still remembered the experience vividly — there were none of the amnesiac patches which occur in an alcoholic drunk. And in reliving those sixteen hours in my mind, I realized that something irreversible, even final, had happened to me. All my certainties had been smashed in one blow, my intellectual and emotional world was in shambles as a result of one brief contact with this supra-rational, unhuman 'Presence'. And the most infuriating thing about it all was that it was impossible to convey what it was like in any comprehensible manner to someone who had not had the experience; you either knew or you didn't. There was no midway position. And if you *did* know, that knowledge was terrifying in its implications for your daily life. For almost all human activity was reduced in importance to the level of playing with toys.

Of course I did not rush out into the street and proclaim to the passers-by that I had just conducted a most instructive interview with God. Nor did I feel I had inherited the mantle of the new Messiah. In fact what obsessed me most was the disturbing connection between my experience and what I had so far spurned under the all-embracing label of 'self-deluding religious mumbo-jumbo'. I was vaguely aware that certain aspects of that sixteen-hour happening had been previously recorded by other people, most of them amorphously called 'mystics'. William James had written about such experiences and modern psychiatry had devoted considerable attention to certain types of schizophrenic perception which were not entirely dissimilar to my own.

The only external ratification I could find however was back in the land of my birth: India, the country I had rejected. For this is how Shankara*, a young man in his mid twenties, described the *Brahman* hundreds of years ago: 'The *Brahman* is neither existent nor non-existent and is both statical and dynamical, indescribable and un-nameable ... is neither spirit nor being, neither material nor immaterial, is everywhere and nowhere, pervades everything and everyone, the true god within each and every one of us ...'

And Gaudapada, Shankara's teacher, describes the real 'I' in these terms: 'This self as unseen is unrelationable, ungraspable, indefinable, unthinkable, unspeakable and the extinction of the appearance, the quiescent, the good and the One.'

Clearly then the experience I had had was not a drunken lunatic dream or a megalomaniacal hankering for cosmic power. Good or bad, other men at other times had experienced the 'Presence' and my limited reading of the Upanishads confirmed that there were various schools of metaphysical thought which provided differing deductions and explanations of the phenomenon.

Equally clearly, I now understood why Western philosophers had in the main dismissed the claims of Vedantic metaphysics. Because the origin from which all Upanishadic schools start is not susceptible to proof: it is fact, raw data, and without that accepted data, all systems fall to nothing. Also, this experience was not easily attainable and had very little affinity with the pious religiosity of priests, Christian or otherwise. Conceptually, the *Brahman* was a far tougher proposition than 'God the Benign Father'. Thus it was easy to parody the *Brahman*. For to get a composite description of this thing, all you had to do was put 'non' in front of every conceivable human attribute and *voilà*, there you have the *Brahman* packaged in perfect syntax. And since proponents claimed that 'experience', not belief, was of the essence, there was no way of disputing the existence of the 'Presence' if it hadn't chosen to come your way. And of course those to whom it had would be expectedly jealous of their membership of an elite club and were therefore unlikely to give the game away, even if it did consist of a gigantic hoax. So they had it both ways — if you knew, then that was all there was to it, nothing further to be said. If you didn't know, there was no way of telling you.

I knew these arguments, I had used them myself. I had dismissed the whole business of religion and mysticism as sorcery, cheap tricks to hoodwink the ignorant and unperceptive masses. But now the tables were turned and I had perceived a phenomenon whose existence I had once categorically denied. Nor was that all. I had put

*See *History of Indian Philosophy*, Surendranatha Dasgupta, Cambridge University Press.

my faith in Western empiricism, syllogistic reasoning: I had painstakingly built up an intellectual apparatus which I believed was superbly capable of processing external reality and arriving at wholesome, unsuperstitious truths. And now that very empiricism dictated that I treat my experience seriously, and deduce from it a system of beliefs, which if sincerely practised would demolish the entire mental superstructure I had erected for myself since adolescence.

I realized that my rejection of India and all religious values per se was an emotional process which I had cloaked in intellectual jargon. It was connected with mother and my exposure to certain odious aspects of the fabric of Bengali society. My denial had then been total, in the hope that I could purge myself of these unwholesome attitudes and build anew. I had chosen the easier alternative of massing it all together in one lump without bothering to sieve out what was relevant and valid in that society from the corrupt and degrading. The ferocity with which I had screamed out against mother had made me deaf to subtler sounds. I had committed the intellectual sin of seeing main-line connections where they did not always exist — mother's passivity with Indian obsequiousness, the common belief in fatalism with Hindu dogma, parental authoritarianism with the social ethos. Experiences which had mutilated me emotionally were immediately linked in my mind with the larger social canvas: a specific grievance was always caused by inexorable social forces which I or anyone else had little power to change. This provided apparent intellectual respectability for my actions and opinions, but in fact it was a crude structure, for the dishonesty lay in taking the wish for the fact.

Not that the society I had spurned was an idyllic one. In many respects it was the most repulsive social structure I had ever encountered. Hypocrisy was a national institution and perversions of true doctrine an endemic disease. If you could persuade the masses about the reality of the *Brahman* (as generations of self-seeking Hindu priests had done), then it was unnecessary to *do* anything about poverty, exploitation and hunger. From the subtle metaphysics of Brahminic paradox, where worldly action was not at a premium, to commitment and acquiescence in divine pre-determination was a short step. Especially if the masses do not read Sanskrit and the leaders of society are invested with holy power, the sanctification of hereditary hierarchy that caste enshrines. Invoke the Vedas and the Upanishads, which no one has read and no one ever will, and you have the ultimate pain-killer — if life is hard today, don't worry, these things are not really 'real', and anyway there is always tomorrow, the afterlife, where you will reap rich rewards for all the holy things you have done in this one. If parents appear to be doing wrong, don't you dare mutter a word of disrespect, for they are the earthly incarnations of the Divine Godhead, fit only for zealous worship and unquestioning obedience.

But the grass was not all green on the other side of the fence. I had abandoned India with fierce dogmatism, only to discover that Western society was not free from worms either. Empiricism, reason, belief in human life and individual dignity, were not always carried out in practice. Hypocrisy was not an oriental monopoly, nor was exploitation, intellectual arrogance and ruthless rejection of ambiguity. Shallow assertion and gaudy pomposity were features of *Man*, not necessarily of any one system.

My experience under LSD unsettled my intellectual structure. But it also did a good deal more. It totally destroyed my faith in the *possibility of certainty*. It reintroduced fundamental questions in my mind which I had to try and reanswer from first principles — the purpose of Art, the conception of progress, the commitment to humanism, prescriptions of remedies to social malaise. I could no longer hold a view with any degree of dogmatism. Lacking the courage to forsake this 'unreal' world in quest of 'true reality', LSD made me truly humble for the first time in my life.

It was precisely because I had taken LSD (in fact I am sure that the 'trip' was a preparation for what was about to happen — I had swallowed that capsule a little over six months before she died) that all those rituals connected with mother's death assumed a spectral aspect. My body was an embarrassment, my tears obscene, I would have wanted to be somewhere else. I knew a little more but not nearly enough. Mother was dead and I was crying. The lower depths from which those tears welled were too murky for the pristine eyes around me.

As I looked at those dry griefless faces, waves of guilt swept over me. I had no right to weep. It was I who had forsaken the parental home, inflicted pain, squandered my substance in riotous living. I was the Prodigal, they the elder sons, dutifully attending. All these years I hadn't given a moment's thought to mother while they had been selflessly caring, ministering to her needs. I had violated her wishes, desecrated family tradition, lived among 'red-faced' heathens and broken bread with non-Brahmin *mlechhas* (untouchables). I had done what no son should ever do — flung back mother's love in her face and unleashed terrible sorrow in her heart. And now that she was dead, did I have the cheek to cry?

The question reverberated in my mind but Pilate would not wait for an answer. Instead my eldest brother asked, 'Are you going to observe the period of *ashauj*?'*

---

*The ascetic observance of mourning rituals for eleven days following a death and culminating in a great *puja* ceremony, the *sraddha*, which consecrates the departed soul to heaven.

There were many queries hidden in that single one and the innuendoes did not escape me. I looked at my two elder brothers and their faces set the old battle raging once again. They were both unshaven, wore unstitched cloth and walked barefoot. Ritual dictated that they sleep on the bare stone floor every night, cook their own unsalted, unspiced vegetarian food on a portable coal cooker once a day and do without oil and soap in their baths. Shreds of handwoven cloth would have to suffice for towels; cigarettes were out and so was any other form of 'luxury'.

No, they were neither heroes nor martyrs but simply the senior members of an orthodox Brahmin family. In that short simple question I was being asked to redefine myself all over again. Would I, as the youngest son of our dear departed mother, care to join this spartan clan? Would I conform to custom and abide by ritual? Or had I become too anglicized to perform these last sacred rites to sanctify her soul? Mother would have wanted me to do it, in her present non-terrestrial abode she would be comforted to know that I had done so. Did I not have the least bit of feeling left in my heart? Had I no respect for the last unspoken wish of the hallowed dead?

The gross and unholy truth was that I had not. Mother was irretrievably dead; for me she had no other existence. Even my LSD experience had not prompted belief in a personal soul or in a life hereafter. Whatever the Ultimate Reality, it was not human. I was quite convinced that nothing survived after death, certainly not in any form we know or can comprehend. All this ritual was degrading because it shifted the raison d'être from oneself to the other person. It externalized essentially interior and personal needs, and the *sraddha* ceremony was a huge cathartic ablution — the easy way out of having to bear the haunting demands of memory. To say I was keeping *ashauj* for mother's sake would be an indecent travesty of truth. For I believed in no such thing.

Of course I could have joined the circus, in the same mischievous way as I had done by getting married in an Anglican church in London to the strains of 'Lead Kindly Light Amidst The Encircling Gloom ...' But there was one signal difference between a church wedding and the keeping of *ashauj* leading up to the final *sraddha* ceremony. And this is where personal vanity and my commitment to comfort intervened decisively. On the former occasion I had worn a Savile Row suit, imbibed large quantities of alcohol throughout the day and had been subject to no deprivation or assault other than the aesthetic one of having to expose myself to the high nasal pitch of the vicar's sermonic voice. On the latter occasion, if I agreed to be part of the performance, I would have to be dressed as a mendicant clown, nurse an empty belly and mumble Sanskrit *mantras* for hours on end. And most pertinently I would be the unproud bearer of a wholly shaven head* — a brown Yul Brynner, without his physiognomy or his stature, and no Hollywood cameras anywhere in the vicinity. So even with my penchant for surrealism and 'the Theatre of the Absurd', I declined to answer my brother's question in the affirmative.

But surrealism and vanity were not the only deterrents. That bizarre church wedding provided more than an analogy to the ensuing tableaux. It institutionalized the gulf between me and my family and opened up a chasm which could not be wished away with polite words and reconciliatory embraces. By marrying an English girl I had lost my caste and become impure. And in that impure state, the book of rules would not allow me to perform the *sraddha* ceremony and consecrate my mother's soul. But privileged mortal that I was (a Brahmin by birth) I could be received back into the fold if I were to do penance (*prayashchitta*) for having crossed the black waters (the oceans separating India from all other lands) and eaten food with the *mlechhas* (untouchables). And most crucial of all, if I were to perform the purifying rituals for having cohabited† with a European woman, I would be revarnished enough to shine forth once more with true Brahminic radiance. My soul would be cleansed and I would be worthy of offering *puja* at the *sraddha*.

But of course I was quite content with the state of my soul as it was. And I had no intention of doing 'penance' for an act I did not consider sinful. For were I to undergo the purification ritual, I would be effectively repudiating my marriage and acknowledging a system of beliefs which I found violently repulsive. I had naively believed that all this would have been taken for granted by now. But the astounding thing was that it was not and my family did expect an eleventh-hour conversion to be precipitated by mother's death. They knew I could ignore didactic sermonizing. But could I have become so desiccated emotionally as to trample the sacred memory of mother underfoot? To them the question was stark and simple: In this critical hour, which side are you on?

For me however, the situation throbbed with ambiguity and came menacingly close to a self-flagellating inquisition. I had married an English girl, seven years older than myself, a widow with two

---

*A day before the *sraddha* ceremony, *all* hair from the waist upwards is shaved off. Then the victim has to immerse himself in the holy Ganges for some considerable time, to wash all impurities away.

†Hindu ritual, as distinct from Indian law, does not recognize any marriage not performed according to the sacred rites before a burning fire. By cohabiting with a white girl you contaminate yourself but technically remain unmarried, no matter what other kind of vow you have taken. And since no religious ceremony can be conducted between two people from different castes, no Hindu can technically get married to a non-Hindu and have his marriage accepted by the pundits.

children. Any *one* of these factors would have earned outright social denunciation in India. Combined, they projected the picture of an ogre. At best the man who married such a woman could be pitied as a demented derelict. At worst he was a subversive traitor, to be shunned with the same hysterical terror as one would a plague-ridden syphilitic. I was aware of these responses, I knew of them when I made the decision. But I had insisted to myself that the condemnation of Indian society did not matter to me; what my family felt about my actions was of no consequence. How far was that really true? How honest had I been with myself and how much of it was histrionic bravado?

I was married six months before mother's death. But I did not inform my family till I reached Calcutta, three days after she had been burnt on the pyre. Did I withhold the information because — as I had told myself at the time — I wanted to save her pain? Or was I intimidated by the vehement social opprobrium with which I expected the announcement to be greeted? The very fact that these questions pressed themselves indicated that the issue was far from resolved in my mind. Self-justifying rationalization was a crude and inept way of concealing weakness, the inability to practise defiantly what one professed to believe.

My mother's obsessive goal for my life had been to see me safely married to 'a nice Bengali Brahmin girl'. In the last ten years, every time I visited India the subject of my marriage had formed the staple fare of all conversations between us. Brides had been selected, middlemen employed, horoscopes examined, and once even provisional preparations for a whirlwind wedding had been made. The objective, as I saw it, was twofold. The primary one was to prevent exactly the kind of marriage I finally did make — with all the attendant degradations of loss of religious status, the prospect of half-caste children and social ostracism of the family as a whole. The second objective was less socially and religiously imperative but figured strongly enough for my mother: if I married a Bengali girl, the chances of my returning to live in India would be hugely enhanced.

For my part I had no objections at all to marrying 'a nice Bengali Brahmin girl'. But no such girl I met even remotely approximated to the kind of person I wanted for a wife. And I was adamantly against the system of arranged marriage, where adjustment, compromise, 'making the best of what you've got' were the critical determinants, rather than freedom of choice, love and volitional compatibility. I was prepared to accommodate myself to mother's conditions provided the person in question met my requirements as well. But not otherwise. So I had long reluctantly resigned myself to the idea that when and if I finally did get married, it would cause her great pain. (The chances of meeting a single Bengali Brahmin girl, with whom I would share a mutual attraction, in London or elsewhere in the

Western world, would surely approach the absolute zero.) I accepted this as a fait accompli and it may even explain why I wrecked several previous relationships just before they were about to dock safely into harbour.

But then when I heard that mother was on her death-bed, I decided, with some prompting from my wife, to fly out with her and our two children. Why? If the news of our marriage would have caused mother pain six months earlier, when she was physically in good shape, would she not now feel even worse in her critical condition? Six months previously, in fact all my adult life, I had felt that there was no possibility of persuading her to accept my marriage with a European girl. Mother's prejudices and religious bigotry were ineradicable. If I had not been able to persuade her to my way of thinking some fifteen years ago (and I did try then), what chance now in the very winter of her life? So if she was not going to change her mind, if she would be crushed by sorrow, why tell her something with which she could never come to terms?

I believe my decision was dictated by several factors, the principal one being a feeling that finally mother would not condemn *anything* I did. A message on a letter or a telegram does not carry the same defiant impact as physical presence. Printed words may be argued against, repudiated even, but not so the human voice, the touch of loving hands or the breaching of absence with a tender look in the eye. If I could hold her in my arms and if she could see my wife, however strong her reproof, it would be over-ridden — we would both be accepted. I was her darling son, I could do no wrong. If she was at death's door, all the more reason for silly old religious and social taboos to be waved aside.

The threat that she might leave my life forever induced panic. I realized that I wanted, needed, mother's approval. At the very last moment I hungered for her total unconditional love, just as I had always done. I needed to have her love for everything I was, warts, wife and all. I could not possibly deceive her on her death-bed, even by omission. I nursed the unwavering conviction that the insensate curtain of her senility would be drawn aside; she would recognize me and I would give her that last gift of love which I had unceasingly had from her. The final reunion would seal us together; nothing could or would come between her and me.

But she had left without a word of farewell and I would never know what her final verdict would have been. The rasping calls of memory would echo in my mind, guilt would be my permanent companion, there would be no absolution at the end of the road. Not right and wrong or morality and ethics but the simple everlasting issues of pain and love and suffering would haunt me in my dreams. I would see her pleading face, the unshed tears in her eyes, and I would inherit in my heart a load which she had borne all her life. The gnawing terror of uncertainty would stalk me mercilessly; every act would be open to question, every gesture a mirage quest for final commitment. Mother was dead and I was born again. But this time there would be no breast-feeding, no shelter from the gales of a monstrous and unloving world. I would have to do it all alone.

And alone I was for the rest of my stay in Calcutta. For though I was close to my wife, albeit in a fragile and tenuous manner, I could not expect her to comprehend the nuances of feeling and response that coursed through me. All those other faces, tied to me by blood and custom and history, were so many strangers, intruders in the dark, with whom no communication was possible. We spoke a different language, our assumptions were divided by a world and a culture. And the impossible burden of silence lay on me: I knew what they felt and why they thought the way they did. But there was no one with whom I could share the ravages of the dialectical storm raging inside me.

Yet once I had absolved my family from the responsibility of choice, the way ahead was surprisingly free of acrimony. By refusing to do *prayashchitta* and observe *ashauj*, I had taken the whole load upon myself; they were not involved. My sin was on my head; there was nothing they could do about it nor were they contaminated by any of my actions. Had I forced the issue though, insisted on performing the religious ceremony in my 'impure' condition, flaunted my English wife and press-ganged her into joining me in all the various rituals, there would have been confrontation, and the foul smell of bigotry might well have poisoned the whole proceedings.

As I had no dual feelings, the clash was avoided. My family received us with proverbial Indian hospitality. Their kindness and generosity overwhelmed my wife, who had been apprehensive all along about the possible outbreak of hostilities between me and my brothers. It would have been a crucial test of our marriage. For if I had been forced to choose, where would my ultimate loyalty lie? If my brothers insisted that I was welcome only if I did not bring my wife and our children into the house at the *sraddha* ceremony, what would I have done? Of course I had decided in advance that I would not recant, that my marriage was final, my commitment to the anti-ritualistic stance total. But the question remains, since my resolution was fortunately not put to the test.

There wasn't a trace of discrimination (which is more than I can say about some 'liberals' in this country) in the way all four of us were taken into the house. This made me rethink my preconceived notions about the exclusive hauteur of Bengali consciousness. I had cause to wonder if I had been all that objective in my analysis of the besieged Brahmin psyche. How impenetrable were religious taboos outside specifically religious occasions? I would be wrong to give the impression that *I* was forgiven for all I had done. But a clear distinction was made between my actions (however wrong they were) and their results. Neither my wife nor our two children were penalized for my misdeeds — and indeed misdeeds they were thought to be. They were treated, in the best traditions of Western liberalism, as individuals, to be appraised, liked or disliked on their own merits. And since my wife possesses some innate Indian characteristics, like demureness, grace and apparent docility, she was instantly taken into the bosom of the family with the same facility as if I had married 'a nice Bengali Brahmin girl'.

My family's response to me personally was far more complex and ambiguous. As a favourite son of our departed mother, I had earned their life-long resentment, perhaps even jealousy — even though my eldest brother was now a grandfather twice over, and my second brother, at forty-three, was shortly about to retire from the Indian Air Force. I was the one who had got away with murder. I had violated tradition yet had suffered no retribution. I had done what I liked when I liked, yet my parents (yes, both of them) had always pampered me, treated me as something special, as if I were a hothouse plant, rare and vulnerable. I had been protected and indulged — none of the labour but all the prizes.

If they had fought me as a brother, as an equal, I believe the situation would have been resolved long ago, one way or another. But there was another parameter, the insidious mystique of 'Age' which determined their feelings and responses. As older sons of the family — my eldest brother is twenty-two years my senior, old enough to be my father — they were expected to be guardians of my well-being. Overt competition was ruled out by the ethos. They had to accept the role of protectors, and yet the emotional tensions remained.

I was aware of these tensions and I had always wickedly exploited this duality in their feelings towards me. I willingly fell into the role of a 'little brother', the vulnerable fledgling in desperate need of the strength and wisdom of older birds. I am not even sure that I could have ever defied them face to face. But the one weapon I used rendered them defenceless — my pen. Over all those years I had lived at home, I had been brewing the most subversive stew in my mind, while on the outside I was relatively acquiescent and conventionally respectful. When my book* came out they were knocked off course. Was this the way to treat all their love and concern? Did I have no sense of decency, no respect for privacy? If I had felt this way about them, what was the point of putting it all down in public print? Couldn't I have talked with them first?

Of course my answer would be, 'No, I couldn't', and besides they

My God Died Young — an autobiography. Hutchinson, London; Harper & Row, New York, 1968.

wouldn't have understood or listened anyway. But I am a prejudiced witness. Truth lies somewhere out there, and I own no freehold rights over these estates.

Their reaction towards me oscillated between pitying condescension and awe. No Indian ever thinks his culture inferior. He will pretend, doff his cap, make contemptuous allowances for alien inadequacies, but in the core of his being he is firmly convinced that nothing transcends his world-view. 'There are no new things to be done, no new thoughts to be thought. All that is good and wise and brilliant and original, it has all been done here, long, long ago. No one can teach us anything. The red-skins may have come and overruled us, but they were ignorant barbarians all the same.'

This smooth confidence is invulnerable as long as the 'them' and 'us' dichotomy exists. But when someone crosses the floor, and takes with him the privileges that 'we' have always claimed to be 'ours', and then attacks 'us' with the instruments that 'they' have perfected, the war becomes tense and maudlin in one breath. Sentimental seductions are attempted; sobbings of the throat, invocations of filial and fraternal piety are piled on high. Then when these fail, outright denunciation, threats of cultural excommunication, the harrowing spectre of not being regarded as an Indian at all, are all paraded with the exquisite grace of inquisitional sensibility. Failure at this stage reduces the protagonist to hysterics — random throws which carry the odour of frenzy.

One day in private conversation within the family, I would be called 'brilliant'. On another, in the presence of relatives and friends, I would be informed that I was a liar and a harlot, time-serving opportunist and licker-upper of certain posterior crevices of the Western world. My book was a gala of falsehoods, an attempt to capitalize on anti-Indian feeling in the occident, a cheap way to climb the ladder up to a literary and financial haven.

There was a heartening duplicity in all this. 'It is good and proper that a member of the *Chakravarti* family has earned recognition in the West. After all, that is only to be expected. However, we must not talk about how he came about such accolades. Because that whole book was a fabrication, nothing that he says in there has the faintest connection with the way things are round here. But we all know that of course. It is a pity that this kind of book ever gets published, that Westerners are given such misleading descriptions of India. We are not just a land of snake-charmers and fakirs, you know. We are the proud legatees of a very ancient civilization.'

(Like Aristotle Onassis was a legatee of Socrates?)

On the invitation card to the *sraddha* ceremony, my name appeared at the bottom of a list of three, as befitted my station; my two elder

brothers preceded me. Despite my 'impure' condition, I was though
to be worthy enough to act as one of the hosts to our four-hundred
odd guests who were invited. On the day before the feast, all twenty o
us (the immediate family) trooped down to the banks of the Ganges
My brothers had their heads shaved, their arm pits scraped and thei
hirsute chests reduced to a suitably depilated and mournful
condition. I agreed to go half way out in this macabre drama and my
shoulder-length locks were shorn to short back and sides. *Pujas* were
offered, immersions performed and Mother Ganga received the
discarded impurities of three recently orphaned sons with her usual
benign holiness.

On the day of the *sraddha* ceremony, my wife, our children and I
arrived at the family house at seven in the morning (we were staying
with friends). The only request my brother made was that neither I
nor my wife should smoke openly in public. We agreed and sought
refuge in the bathroom at odd intervals. No other restriction was
imposed, no other observance of ritual expected. I gave in to one small
custom which didn't call for extensive readjustment of my
convictions — to do *pranam** to elders on first meeting. Apart from
this we both dressed in Bengali clothes. My wife had her hair parted in
the middle, with vermilion powder sprinkled over the parting.† She
wore a sari and conducted herself with the pliancy one would expect
from a bride newly inducted into the house. Surprisingly, most of our
guests thought our two blonde children were the product of my loins
and they received the same exalted welcome as would a progeny of
mine.

The visitors started to pour in by mid-morning: relatives, friends,
well-wishers and their accompanying broods of children. The
women wore gold-brocaded saris and glittering jewellery, while the
men were attired in silk and muslin, with leather sandals on their feet.
Half a dozen hired cooks were at work on hastily improvised coal
cookers in the courtyard in front of the house. Long rows of tables and
benches were set, banana leaves were washed and spread out (these
serve as plates from which the food is eaten by hand), clay tumblers
and brass jugs held at the ready. Greetings and *pranams* were
exchanged in abundant profusion. Younger participants in the
festivity sneaked off into corners and stole the odd embrace from a
member of the opposite sex so disposed; mothers talked solicitously to

*_Pranam_ — touching the other person's feet with one's right hand and then bringing it
in contact with one's forehead. It is a kind of greeting ritual, not dissimilar in its
function to a Western handshake, though the symbolism underlines once again the
mystique of 'Age', as only a junior does it to a senior and not the other way round.

†The vermilion powder on the parting indicates that a woman is married and her
husband is still alive. Widows are not permitted to use the powder. In my wife's case, as
she had been a widow once, and as widows in India don't — in general — remarry, the
ritual and reality were somewhat at cross purposes.

each other of impending births and marriages. Men conferred in grave tones about stocks and shares or the state of the nation. I nodded, bowed, smiled and *pranamed,* drifting from one cluster of people to another, *de trop* in the very house in which I was born, at the *sraddha* ceremony of the mother who gave me birth.

Of course the principal performers in the religious ceremony were my two elder brothers, though my sisters-in-law joined in peripherally. My wife, poor girl, was not allowed into the holy enclave. So she stood a decorous distance away and took photographs of the pageant. I *was* in fact allowed in, though not permitted to touch the *Vedi* — the holy of holies, consecrated ground.

What struck me was the sheer irrelevance of the whole performance. The rituals lasted for over six hours. Presents were made to Brahmins; priests were handsomely rewarded; endless Sanskrit *mantras* were intoned. Calves, bedsteads and banana plants were given away; holy water sprinkled at intervals of ten minutes, sandalwood paste plastered over faces and huge fires lighted with costly milk-fat.

Yet no one in the whole assembly understood a single word of what they were all parroting. Not one person took the slightest interest in discovering the meaning of these rituals, the symbolism intended, the purpose of all this activity. They had fasted the whole day, yet they couldn't explain why an empty stomach was preferable to a full one. They coughed and sputtered as the noxious fumes swam into their faces, yet they did not have the faintest idea of the significance of 'Fire' to those early Aryans who had formulated this entire rigmarole. Most devastating of all, they did not even ask themselves the simple, obvious questions: 'What has all this got to do with mother? How are feelings affected? What good will it do her, wherever she may be?'

Like robots they repeated the words, sleepwalking they sprinkled holy water — the priests dictated, they obeyed. No question, no analysis, just the rigorous adherence to custom. It was all so devoid of humanity, this mechanical execution of a set of rites. As I looked on with a horrified fascination, I remembered the story of another such ritualistic occasion when a couple about to be married had gone through half the ceremony before somebody discovered that the priest had got hold of the wrong book — the *mantras* they had been mumbling were really meant for a *sraddha* ceremony.

I wondered if anyone would take a moment off to think of mother, what her life had been, how she had suffered. True, there was a large framed photograph of the Grande Dame in one of the rooms, before which a large group of hired musicians sang holy songs, which were then amplified over the loudspeakers so that everyone in the house and outside could hear. But was it really being done for her? Or were they congratulating themselves, boasting of the display they were putting on for their guests? In all that fun and feasting, I missed my mother. All I could see in the eyes of my brothers was relief.

When the day was done, when the hired cooks had been sent home and servants masticated betel-nut leaf in the kitchen, when the children slept and mother's room was shut to prying eyes, when the Captain and the King's men had departed, and the clatter of jewellery and the sounds of holy music had sunk low into the night, there was a strange hush in the house once more. Her spirit moved over the still waters of memory, the smell of incense lingered.

It was then that the stories from The Family began. 'Do you know how mother died? For all these years, the only one she would ever talk about was you. Sometimes she would behave like a child, she would want to cable you and fly out by the next plane. None of us mattered at all. At first she wanted you to marry "a nice Bengali girl". (Pity you didn't tell us about that *entanglement* you had at college. Father was very influential in this city, you know, he would have arranged something.) But later, she would have been happy to see you married to anyone at all, even a creature with four legs.'

My wife was a witness to all this. But it was spoken in Bengali, which she didn't understand, and I didn't feel obliged to translate. For the first time since I had come 'home', tears rolled down the faces round me while my eyes remained dry.

Then, 'You should thank your lucky stars you didn't have to see her at the last. Your memory is pure, you will always remember her as she used to be. But if only you had looked at her, if you had had to nurse her even for a day ... large lumps of flesh, soft as putty, plucked out by hand, bones showing in places, bed sores — do you know what bed sores are? — all over her back. She couldn't recognize anyone, not even her own sons. She went out of her mind quite some time ago. Mumbling your name all the time. No, she was not the mother you knew, not at the end. Thank God you didn't see her that way.'

Instantly, my old friend 'Guilt' appeared by my side, invisible, disconcerting. But I wasn't going to be condemned without a trial. 'How am I responsible for all this? Why implicate me? I didn't create the bed sores on mother or bring on her senility.'

The Family replied, 'No, no, of course you didn't. You will go far in life. You have been published abroad, you have ambition. And that is no bad thing. Just that mother wanted you with her, she was always talking about you. She used to store things away for you — oh, don't forget to take the gold bangles back with you, she left them specially for your wife, *whoever* she might be. And she just wanted to see you, you know. Put her hand on your head and pat your cheeks. Old women get like that sometimes, they like to see their sons once in a while. Of course you were away, and you were busy. But you really should have seen her when we put her on the funeral pyre. Poor mother!'

PART TWO

3

The Condemned Playground

I remember I was seized with sudden
panic ... and for one endless sound I
was overwhelmed by an absurd wish t
draw back, to give it all up, to escape;
but a huge gulf separated me ... a
gulf that had grown inordinately wide
while I was crossing it, so that now I
could not plumb its depth...

MICHEL BUTOR, *Passing Time*

I stand between two worlds. I am at
home in neither, and I suffer in
consequence.

THOMAS MANN, *Tonio Kröger*

It was the kind of Odyssey which was likely to have its Joycean
apotheosis in a lavatory bowl. The objective was laudable but the
process of execution seemed to entail more than its requisite share of
contact with human imbecility and venal ineptitude.

A young Indian called Esbee, with shoulder-length locks and a
sharp triangular beard, was travelling en famille — with wife Pamela
and their two children — from London to his birthplace in India: no
doubt a species of journey which thousands of other Indians regularly
undertake without feeling compelled to record it for posterity. But
there were a few exceptional features to this particular expedition:
one was the fact that Esbee was a writer cast in an obsessively
autobiographical mould; and the other was the result of an attempt at
economy which had induced this family to travel, inadvertently, with
the wretchedest airline on planet earth.

Arbitrary stops in the middle of deserts and sheikhdoms, without
alcohol or air-conditioning in the terminal building; hours-long
roastings inside the grounded plane, with two loos out of four not
functioning; the incessant whine of babes-in-arms, snot dripping
down their noses as they were brazenly breast-fed in public by their

Indian mothers — these were just some of the features of that unforgettable twenty-six-hour journey, at the end of which the four of them finally came down to earth.

As the door of the aircraft opened, Calcutta heat came at them like a sudden rush of steam in a sauna bath. The sharp light stabbed their eyes, the viscous air stank of gasoline and sweat. The two little girls clambered down from the plane, clinging to their mother. Heat, light and sound, the Babel of voices around, dazed them. In a little while they began to cry.

Esbee, weighed down by a large portmanteau in each hand, walked on ahead and slammed his passport on the counter. The man on the other side looked up after an eternity and pronounced, 'Breetish'. Esbee nodded, his eyes shot with sweat, shirt pasted to skin and his temper perilously close to explosion.

'You are Bengali?' the man asked.

'So what?' Esbee threw back.

'Nothing, nothing. No need to make shouting.'

'Every damn need, I reckon. I'll bloody well make all the shouting I want. We've been through this once already, and that took three hours. How many days will it take here, eh?'

Stirred by the commotion, the boss, seated at a desk some ten feet away, rose leisurely from his chair, spat out a mouthful of red betel-nut juice and ambled over to the side of his colleague. 'What is matter?'

'This gentleman make a lot of shouting, sar. I was enquiring ...' the subordinate stammered.

'Now look here mister ...' the boss started saying, as his eyes fell on the passport. 'Breetish?' he queried, just as his underling had done. Inspecting eyes roamed over Esbee's shoulder-length hair and then peered at the photograph on the table. 'Heepy man,' the boss finally concluded, staring his victim in the eye. 'This picture not have long hair.'

At this point, Pamela and the kids joined Esbee. And a sudden transformation took place in those inquisitorial faces. 'You have English wife?' the boss demanded.

'Yes,' Esbee replied.

'Your own children these are?'

'What the hell has that got to do with you?'

'Now mister, mister ... I tell you ...'

'You tell me nothing,' Esbee shouted. 'I want to see the officer in charge of this outfit. *Now*. You go and get him. Or else I'll shout the roof off this building. Do you understand? I want to speak to your head man. Right now.'

A small group of indigenous bystanders had gathered round them by now, full of homely curiosity, eyeing the little girls as if they were animals in a zoo. No harm was meant of course. Only a dark wall of sweaty half-stripped bodies pressed forward, hands tugged at the strands of blond hair — just to make sure they were real — and a loud drone of incomprehensible sounds buffeted their ears. The youngest child, Henrietta, not yet five, started wailing. 'I want ... to go home ... mummy ... I want to go home ...' Tears flooded down her cheeks, while hiccupy sobs broke up the words coming out of her mouth. The older girl, Susannah, stood silent, a look of petrified horror strung across her face.

'Get these people away from here,' Esbee screamed hysterically. 'Or else I'll put the British High Commissioner onto you.' Such threats were futile of course and he was beginning to comprehend the meaning of impotence. He could not even protect his own daughters from being fingered by a crowd of rustic imbeciles. And that in his native land, the very city in which he had spent the first nineteen years of his life.

'*Hato, hato* [Get away, get away],' the boss boomed, insinuating the tone of a cowboy herding cattle. The wooden baton lashed out at a few bodies around, the boots of officialdom struck spindly shins and the acquiescent crowd withdrew a little, bovine grins pasted on every mouth.

Shame hit him hard, he was cornered, Esbee felt a sickening disgust.

He knew these things went on, he had witnessed many such scenes in his youth. But never before had he been the *cause* of any such incident, never willingly subjected his fellow humans to being treated like beasts in a jungle. They knew no better, it was not their fault. And yet ...? What of the two small girls, neither of whom deserved such treatment either? What of his wife, what of his own stretched nerves? How many sides of a question can you look at in a glance. Who was responsible? How should he act?

As manna in the desert, a young man in army uniform strode authoritatively up to the group just then. He was in his mid twenties, wore thick horn-rimmed spectacles and sported a pencil moustache. 'Can I help you, Sir?' he asked, in correct though accented English.

'Yes, I wonder if you could,' Esbee replied. 'I presume you are the officer in charge here?'

'No Sir, I am his assistant. The OC is not here at the moment. Can I help you?'

'Well,' Esbee began, 'I seem to be undergoing some sort of criminal investigation round here. And I can't see why. Especially as we've gone through all this once already, in Bombay.'

'You arrived in Bombay? From where?'

'London.'

By this stage the young man had glanced through the pages in the passport and looked over Pamela and the children. 'You are a "writer", Sir? What is the exact purpose of your visit to Calcutta?'

'I have come to see my mother, she is very ill,' Esbee replied, beginning to be irked once again.

'I see,' the officer said, 'you have the address?'

'Yes, of course. What do you think?'

'No offence, Sir. Just the rules.'

Esbee recited name, address and telephone number.

'That is all, Sir. I am sorry you had a little inconvenience. You will appreciate that because of all these troubles across the border just now, we have instructions about foreigners.'

'But *I* am not a foreigner,' Esbee was about to shout back, but he held his breath just in time. The passport said differently; in the eyes of officialdom, that was what he was, a foreigner.

Some twenty minutes later, when the children were quiet once more and the coolies had been paid off and all the luggage had been packed into the boot of the taxi, Esbee got into the passenger seat in front of the car and muttered mutinously under his breath, 'Bloody good start, I reckon.'

To which Pamela replied, 'Just because you had worked yourself up into a lather. If only you had kept your voice down ... In fact there was no need to show your passport at all. We could have walked through like all the rest.'

'That's what you think,' Esbee countered. 'I bet they'd have stopped us.' But really, he was not all that sure.

The taxi spluttered out of the airport and turned left into a wide macadamized road. The driver, a turbaned Sikh, began conversation in broken English, 'This road not so good at night, sahib. No taxi go here after seven o'clock. But in the daytime like now, very fine. VIP road, very good.'

'And why is it not fine after seven?' Esbee asked.

'Many killing. Also take all money, sahib. Taxi driver no want to get hole in head to make more rupees,' the Sikh replied.

'But what about the police ... don't they?'

'Oh, the police, sahib, they more frightened than taxi driver.'

Esbee began to get an eerie feeling himself. There were few vehicles on the road and scarcely any pedestrians — not quite the way he remembered Calcutta streets to be. But then this was the VIP road, a non-stop dual carriageway — the only one in and around Calcutta — linking Dum Dum airport to the outskirts of the city. The idea was to prevent Very Important People from being exposed to the exotic sights of beggars and buzzing flies immediately on arrival. Hunting round in his memory banks, Esbee figured that the construction of the VIP road had begun at about the time Khruschev and Bulganin visited the bustling metropolis — and that was over a decade ago. And according to the cabbie, it had been completed only some six months earlier. 'Pretty good rate of work for a ten mile stretch of road, wouldn't you say?' Esbee ventured to Pamela.

'You shouldn't be so critical,' she replied. 'It's good that it has been finished at all.'

True, he had no right to be critical. Nearly twelve years ago he had left home, an angry young man, sad and bitter about the society which had spawned him. Eight years later he had adopted British nationality and six months ago he had married an Englishwoman. At each successive turning point in his life he had attempted to sever connections with the land of his birth. It was a continuing process of exorcism, an evil never totally to be expunged. Esbee's innate puritanism ensured that it would be a process which would not terminate, save at the end of his life.

By now they had come to Shambazar junction, on the immediate outskirts of Calcutta. And Esbee was seized by a sudden impulse to visit his old college again, the alma mater. He had so many mixed memories about the place, stirring, nostalgic, verging on sentiment. It would be en route, though not the quickest way to get to their destination. Still, what did it matter? He was here, wasn't he? He had made it. What difference would another five minutes make?

'Drive down to Presidency College, will you?' Esbee told the cabbie.

'Yes, sahib,' the Sikh answered, not quite as ebullient as he had been a little while before.

The two little girls were asleep at the back, the younger one on Pamela's lap, the older one against her shoulder. Sudden heat had lashed them into unconsciousness, and they were spared the revealing sights that reeled past the window. There really was no change, the same shameless deprivation, the old languor, flies, beggars with running sores, garbage piled high on pavements, doleful eyes staring out of skeletal faces, brown, obsequious, at home in despair.

Esbee shut his eyes. He could not pretend to be shocked, as a visiting Westerner could; he had seen it all before. He had no right to be critical, as Pamela had just informed him. He merely writhed within, agonized, trembling with an explosive anger.

'Here Presidency College, sahib,' the Sikh announced, rudely interrupting his reverie. 'Not good get out here, sahib. Plenty trouble.'

Esbee opened his eyes, drew them together into a frown and was about to jump out of the taxi when Pamela intervened. 'You'll have a lot of time to do your sentimental journeys, now that you're here. But please let's get out of these clothes first. I want to wash.'

How like a woman, Esbee thought, and promptly acquiesced. The taxi snorted to life again and started moving off. Just then two khaki-clad soldiers, with rifles on their backs, emerged from the college gates. Is that really so, the old boy thought to himself. But just then his alter ego would not probe for an answer.

A few minutes later, the taxi swerved sharply to the right, climbed onto the pavement and barely missed knocking down an old woman.

'What's the matter?' Esbee shouted. 'Are you drunk or something?'

'No sahib, no drinking me,' the cabbie replied. 'Bomb going off in road.'

Esbee looked back to see a huge cloud of smoke and a stream of pedestrians running towards the direction of their taxi. 'What's going on? What happened?'

'Bomb, sahib. Many bombs every day. Three four men fall down dead. Then military come and do shooting and more people fall down dead. After, they take bodies away. All time like this happening. Bowbazar no good place to come, sahib.'

Such were the facts of life. There was no hysteria in his voice, mere resignation. No use complaining, just make sure you don't get bumped off yourself. In the weeks that followed, Esbee encountered the same response over and over again. The threshold of tolerance, acceptance of violence, pointless loss of life, had risen to an excruciatingly high level.

The man with whom they had arranged to stay was an erstwhile college friend of Esbee's. And such was the close freemasonry in those days, that Esbee, notwithstanding the intervening years, had assured Pamela of a warm welcome from their prospective host. He was in his early thirties, recently inducted into politics, and the scion of a wealthy landowning family in Calcutta, with more than mild aspirations towards aristocratic hauteur. At Presidency College he had been nicknamed 'the Prince'. Whatever other attributes he and his family were renowned for displaying, the quality of offering lavish hospitality was the one most frequently cited. Thus after that gruelling journey, and having telephoned in advance of his impending arrival, Esbee felt he had no need to worry about finding a haven in the house of his long-time friend 'the Prince'.

So when the taxi snorted to a halt under the portico of that huge mansion of a house, Esbee jumped out as if catapulted from a cage. He felt an immense, if perverted, relief at the sight of gate-keepers and messenger boys and turbaned drivers — the kind of entourage he had once known as a boy, representing a style of life he did not now and never ever would have in England. Not that he desired, or even approved of, this archaic world — his response was the purely selfish one of having found the best possible palliatives for his current affliction. Esbee wanted and direly needed a rest. And a multitude of servants go a long way to providing the most egregious kind of rest one can have.

There seemed to be a slight hitch at first however, as none of the servants rushed up to help (as would formerly have been their wont) the taxi driver removed the contents of the boot. Esbee attributed this to the fact that the minions did not remember or know that he was a close friend of their Master's. But Esbee was sure in his mind that once he had met and exchanged hugs and greetings with 'the Prince', all would be well, and the present laggardly behaviour of these courtiers would instantly metamorphose into alert attendance and the proper respect due to a firm and long-absent friend of the family.

But when Esbee disclosed his identity and told the diminutive dhoti-clad figure, the clerk to 'the Prince', to announce their arrival, a very curt reply came back. 'Yes, the Master knows you are here. He requests that you and your family wait in the sitting room.'

This kind of response was unheard of in a Bengali house, especially towards a traveller at the end of a long journey. Add to that the fact that Esbee had been a close friend of 'the Prince' and had indeed been invited to stay in the household, the clerk's reply appeared absurd and unbelievable. 'Obviously, there has been a failure of communication', Esbee thought. And proposed to remedy the situation by simply walking into the house and going up to his friend's room, just as he had always done in his college days.

But Pamela stayed him with a tap on the shoulder. 'Are you sure you want to rush in? He may not want you to go in just like that. After all, it's been a few years since you last saw him ...'

'Of course I can rush in just like that,' Esbee retorted, a trifle bad-tempered. 'You English always judge everything by your own standards. But this is Bengal, remember! The bonds of friendship and the obligations of hospitality are totally different here. You'll see.'

Having made his little speech however, Esbee didn't carry out the implicit threat — he had a few passing doubts himself. Instead he said, 'Come on, we might as well take these things in,' and Pamela, along with the two children, helped him to carry the luggage. Esbee registered, with scarcely concealed disbelief, that none of the servants who had stood around all the while stepped forward to do the job. 'Perhaps they are a bit awed by the blond hair,' Esbee confided to his wife. But his unease was beginning to grow.

Once inside the house, having dumped the suitcases in the hall, Esbee and Co. were shown into the sitting room by the clerk. Here at least he expected that his friend or one of the women of the house would be waiting for the party — since Esbee was accompanied by his wife and children, that would be the normal protocol. But no, there was no one. And Esbee had to collar the clerk to ask where the bathroom and loo were, as he too was about to make an unobtrusive exit.

The clerk pointed to the door at the other end of the room to indicate where it was, and then announced, 'The Master will be down directly.'

Not even a drink of cold water was offered to the children; the loo turned out to be the squatting Indian type. Esbee began to wonder if he had come to the wrong address.

When 'the Prince' walked in half an hour later, he offered his hand to Esbee and said, 'How are you?' in English, and nodded in the direction of Pamela. The children did not rate recognizance.

'We'll be having lunch shortly and then Makhan (the clerk) will take you round to the annexe. I have got several urgent appointments this afternoon and I don't think I shall be able to spare you much time.'

Esbee wondered if he was hallucinating.

During lunch the two older women of the house stood behind 'the Prince', fanning the flies away with a bamboo punkah, ready to obey his smallest command. Since they were widows, they did not join the party at the table. Pamela and the children, unaccustomed to this strange environment and such diabolically rustic manners, did not enter into any conversation. Esbee too was utterly speechless, for very different reasons. Thus, lunch was consumed in total silence but for one exception.

'The Prince' asked Esbee if he would like a beer, to which the guest nodded a grateful assent. One of the women was despatched to fetch some beer and minutes later the reply came back that there was none in the fridge. 'Sorry,' said 'the Prince', 'we seem to have run out.'

Esbee was silently watching himself progress towards a volcanic outburst.

When the time came to be taken round to the annexe, Esbee was no longer making excuses for his one-time friend 'the Prince'. Instead he had to devote all his energies to containing the anger that was boiling within him. Yet the question remained. Why? What was the purpose of such behaviour? Obviously, none of this could be treated as an oversight, it was far too orchestrated and heavy to have been a slip of the mind. But what was the object of the exercise? Esbee could not tell at the time; he had been away from India, and especially Bengal, for far too long. He was not able to dive down into the mire of small minds and hideous inadequacies with easy facility any longer.

That first day, being shown into a one-room flat (with a verandah) in the annexe, Esbee had been humiliated in front of his wife and children. That humiliation had produced a raging tempest of hate and anger. But even then his curiosity did not lie dormant. He wanted to get to the source of this drama, unravel the plot. Of course Esbee did not succeed just then and it was not until a week later that the family were to disdain Princely patronage.

The last straw was heaped on his back when Esbee, on asking to see 'the Prince', was told he could have an interview in three days' time. On the appointed day, Esbee presented himself to the clerk on the dot, and was then kept waiting for half an hour before being ushered into the Royal presence. 'The Prince' did not appear to be heavily garlanded by visitors; indeed there were no secretaries and such like around him either to impress the entrant that affairs of high import had been taking up His Highness's time, so as to account for the half-hour wait.

'I was writing this essay, you see,' the Prince announced, without apology, seated behind a large mahogany desk, 'about the difference between good and evil.' Esbee could not restrain a smile.

The interview lasted all of twenty minutes, at the end of which Esbee felt a great lightness of heart. He decided to leave the establishment the next day, as he had finally found the answer to the question, 'Why?'

It was the old, old story of the frog who wanted to puff itself up into the size of a bull. Only in this case there was the added distortion of a family history made up largely of premature deaths, insanity and suicide — in the best traditions of aristocratic lineage. Esbee realized that instead of anger he should have felt pity, perhaps even contempt. At the worst 'the Prince's reaction should have been treated as a hilarious joke. For what this gentleman was apparently trying to do was impress Esbee with his own Princely, and only latterly acquired political importance, little realizing that our author knew all about noblesse oblige (Lampedusa's novel came to mind), and that pigmies cannot help revealing their height immediately when they begin to strut about. And perhaps it was all to the good, because during that week they stayed in the annexe, Esbee and family were bombarded with the kind of stimuli that are unobtainable anywhere else but in Calcutta.

The contrast between the sepulchral life lived by 'the Prince' in his mausoleum and the pulsating daily deaths on the streets was grotesque to the point of fascination. This was a metaphor for the history of India albeit on a miniature scale. The sheer impassive unconcern among those who lived within the castle walls on the one hand, and the supine acquiescence to a life more degrading than the most neglected species' in the animal kingdom by those who lived outside — this had been the age-old dialectic in the land of the Indus. Now, when the very pace of Time had quickened, it was sad and revealing to see that although the contending parties had changed their apparel and their rhythms, the battle was being fought with the same commitment towards inevitability. 'The Prince' would never accept that his life was precariously balanced on a soap bubble. But neither would his half million fellow citizens, who passed their entire terrestrial existence on the pavements of the city, ever challenge the right of the rich to rule: Fate would take its course. Only now, at the end of the road lay that many splendoured thing called *Death*.

At first it was a feeling, sense of doom, unreality. Then slowly, insidiously, the threat of menace. Little things, small assumptions one makes, were the first casualties. A man strode up to Pamela on the street and told her, 'Do not walk around with your two daughters, you will get killed.' In a bar on a Friday afternoon, the waiter whispered in

Esbee's ear, 'Not go out now sir. Many bullets in street.'

As a visitor, Esbee was inundated with tales of horror and savagery. The usual prescription for the itinerant journalist seemed to be: 'A quick peep into that most recent of tourist attractions, the Refugee Camps, a few civilized parleys with "intellectuals and artists", perhaps an encounter or two with the rich young maidens who were conducting "relief work" and then adieu.' The cardinal precept was, avoid trouble at all costs.

The only redeeming feature about Calcutta was the description of the city given in Bombay. An older myth — 'The real India is in the villages' — had been ousted. By people safely out of its gunshot range, Esbee was told, 'If you want to know what is happening in India right now, go to Calcutta.'

The suggestion made an appeal; Esbee had known Calcutta once upon a time, he could compare, He might not trust his mind, but his instincts seldom failed him. He could sense a situation, smell the air. In a sublimated way, the notion of danger attracted him. If the 'real' India was to be found in Calcutta, he would explore.

But as usual with capsule instructions of this sort, it contained a grain of truth and a massive dose of distortion. For if your olfactory nerves are unaccustomed to noxious odours and you enter a room stuffed full of decomposing bodies, your first reaction will be one of nausea. If you have a tender constitution, you may even faint. All your other senses will be so paralysed that you are unlikely to observe the distinguishing features of one corpse from another. The process of immunization, by which people continue to live in a sick environment, is a slow one. It helps you survive but mangles your responses. This was an advantage, for the outsider may fall a quick victim to the infection, but he will react with greater clarity right up to the moment he succumbs.

Even with that first near-miss with a bomb, Esbee realized that *murder* had become a legitimized vocabulary of retaliation. What had started off as an instrument of political redress had been so frequently and indiscriminately used, that it had now degenerated into a weapon of personal vendetta, cupidity, and a means to deal with even the most minor irritation. Shock was difficult to come by, even among sophisticates. Heinous crimes were accepted, passed by without comment. At a Rotary Club luncheon, the principal speaker made a joke. 'It was pure luck that I made it here this afternoon. There were three bodies lying on the pavement just outside my house when I came out this morning.' The assembly of august businessmen unleashed a volley of appreciative laughter, no one was unduly disturbed and the speaker went on to make his next point. The unnatural had become the norm. Human life, never at a high premium at the best of times in this land of Krishna and Gandhi, had suffered a drastic devaluation. Hunger, disease and destitution, the obscene killers of yore, had been outstripped. Bullets, bayonets and Molotov cocktails were the order of the day.

For death came easily and swiftly in Calcutta. In the single month Esbee was there, over a hundred murders took place in Calcutta alone, according to newspaper reports in the city. A journalist working for the paper which had invited Esbee to write was stabbed to death while returning from his morning shopping. A police sub-inspector was fatally shot; a nineteen-year-old girl was sliced apart by a gang of youths from an opposing faction; a two-year-old infant was thrown out of a first floor window by a bunch of thugs who raided a house. Numerous bombs were thrown; the police, ably aided by the Army, were often incited to return the compliment with machine guns, resulting in the obligatory casualties.

All this was reported in the Press without fuss — single column stories, seldom running into more than four or five inches, titled in small print. No one was particularly exercised, none of these incidents formed the topic of bar or cocktail party conversations. In the air-conditioned offices of the editorial pundits, they never came up for discussion. Esbee was treated to mild censure, with a hint of condescension, when his questions obsessively focussed on the one thing always on his mind: *Death*.

It was a strange feeling, one of persistent apprehension. For the first week in Calcutta, Esbee moved around under a canopy of fear: the kind of fear he had never experienced even in the slums and ghettoes of New York, reportedly one of the most violent cities in the world. Glances from passers-by on the road, remarks from cigarette vendors and taxi drivers, the glum silence of a waiter in a bar — they all seemed to nurse a tightly corked hostility, ready to burst into inhuman retaliation any moment.

Perhaps a good deal of all this was born in his fevered brain; perhaps Esbee was working overtime in his imagination. Perhaps his feeling of being an alien in the very city in which he grew up was totally unrelated to the reality of any external stimulus. Perhaps!

But Esbee was a novelist; he was accustomed to analysing his own reactions. So he wanted to discover something outside himself which would either ratify or demolish his personal vision. And thus he made that sentimental journey back to the alma mater, Presidency College.

Whether he found that clue or not, he could not tell. As with antiques, you need to be a connoisseur to tell the real from the false. But he found a few changes. Where once there were dhoti-clad professors walking down those ancient corridors in somnambulent security, there were now uniformed officers of the Army, with bayoneted rifles and machine guns under their arms. Where once there had been a chemistry laboratory, there were now the tell-tale marks of a bomb explosion, broken window-panes, unhinged doors and empty bottle racks. Where once the Principal sat in stately splendour, there were now Naxalite slogans painted in glaring red: 'Red, redder, ready'; 'Power comes out of the mouth of a gun'.

Newly installed steel collapsible gates punctuated his walk every ten yards. There were no students in sight, the library was deserted. And round every corner, there were these martial law-keepers, brazenly clicking their heels, violating a silence which was steeped in Esbee's mind with the remembrance of times past. A girl called Apu had walked beside him on the green grass, they had stowed themselves away behind a lecture theatre after class, hungering for a kiss. Forgotten sounds echoed again in his mind, the joys of youth and the desecration of hope came flooding back.

Of course the seeds had been sown a long while ago. Only now they had come to grotesque fruition. This land, this culture, these anaemic mentors had brought it all upon themselves. Dead wood deserves the incendiary. Esbee felt perversely elated with the thought that the College he had known, in which he had spent four splendidly hectic years, that College was no more. And from now on, Memory, that flirtatious and quixotic handmaiden of genius, that creature alone would be the guide to a world which was lost forever.

Esbee walked across the field and entered his old department and knocked on the same door before which he had stood all those many years ago after class. That same grey-haired man, now the Head of the Department, said, 'Enter,' in the same indulgent, rickety voice. Almost instantly Esbee was taken into conspiratorial confidence. 'You are now a journalist, I have read about you, and I want to tell you this. They have threatened me several times and I have armed guards in my house, so life is a little quieter than it used to be a few months ago. But if things start up again, they won't let me go. It is either fly or die.' He was sending his son, a school leaver, first to Delhi and then to England. 'Calcutta is no place for a young boy with brains, you understand. Even the handful of conscientious students we have in our department now, we urge them to leave before it is too late.'

Several queries bubble up in Esbee's mind. Why is a physics professor the target of political attack? How come Presidency College (which once correctly claimed to be the Balliol of India) attracts fewer applicants than available seats? And when is it 'too late'? What will happen then that is not happening now?

The Professor, as guru-like as ever, begins to explain. 'These young lads say they want to change society. They want to make revolution and destroy everything. No studies, no books, just *lal jhanda* [red flag]. But what are they going to put in its place? Tell me that. Do they know? Before you demolish a house, you must be sure about the structure you are going to put in its place. Otherwise there will be no roof above your head. Is that good? Tell me that.'

Esbee is unable to reply. He is thirty-two and he too has begun to develop vested interests. But he is unwilling to play truant with his memory. And he remembers the searing anger he felt at eighteen, in this same College, when withered old men had presumed to teach him about Life and Physics and Morals. When daring accepted mores was equated with crime, when perpetuating tradition was held to be a greater virtue than intellectual questing. When the very walls of this old and hallowed institution had thundered disapproval and reprisals to 'a headstrong young boy who has no respect for elders.'

Esbee has also heard of 'revolution'. And he has learnt that when fusty edifices are toppled, no one knows for sure what will take their place. And when the mighty house comes crumbling down, and there is no shelter for anyone, only those who once had a roof suffer. From those who have not, nothing can be taken away.

Esbee knows something of both worlds. He was born in a well-to-do home, he has experienced privilege. Then he cut loose from parental patronage and took to the road. He has known hunger, rooflessness and the cold, fuming hatred of the underdog. His sympathies lie with those who fight rather than with those who accept. And he is curious.

So he wanders over to Coffee House, the favourite haunt of his college days. With relief he notices that time appears to have stood still here. The faces are younger, there are fewer boys in trousers and bush shirts. Tables are no longer segregated; the women call their male colleagues by the familiar *tui* rather than the formal *apni*. Most conversation is in Bengali, hardly a sentence in English. The price of coffee has gone up a little but the old green-topped tables are still there. The room still throbs with the insistent drone of urgent voices; dense clouds of roasted tobacco smoke hang in the air. Waiters lounge around as before; heated debates are still taking place about the fate of the universe: except this time it is in earnest; action at the end of the road.

Not like College at all. Strange that those empty corridors should now be packed with bayonets and machine guns, and here in this noisy bazaar, the devotees of 'Learning' should while away their hours. The contrast is sharp and the reason startling.

Esbee walks over to three young men and asks if he may join them at the table. There is a happy nonchalance in their looks, but no one makes a reply. Esbee pulls up a chair and sits down. 'I used to come here a lot some twelve years ago,' he says in Bengali, by way of introduction. 'Things don't seem to have changed much since then.'

'Oh, but they have *dada**, they most certainly have,' the three of them chorus with a laugh. 'You haven't been around, obviously. Everything has changed. You should ask the Principal of the College

---

*dada — respectful form of address to an older man.

across the road and he will tell you if things are the same.'

'I was a student of Presidency myself and I did notice a few alterations just now.'

'You can say that again. Patrolled by khakis, guarded by dogs at night, barbed wire fencing all over the place — that's the state of the great Presidency College right now.' The boy who makes this speech has a small beard, a scar on his left eye and wears a pair of cracked spectacles. His clothes are unwashed: the shirt bears generous blotches of coffee stains and has no buttons.

'Do you study in Presidency College yourself?' Esbee enquires.

'Yes I do, or used to,' the young man replies. 'The College has been shut for over a year now. No lectures, nothing. Before all this, I was in the Economics department.'

'You mean they have no classes, no exams ...?'

'That's right.'

'Why is that?' Esbee asks.

'Well,' says the Economist, 'it is a long story going back about four years. But the specific reason why they shut up this time was because we went on strike when they wanted to send a boy down for his political activities.'

'Was he a Naxalite?'

'They call everyone that, so what's the difference?'

There is cynicism in his voice, as well as contempt. But no resignation. The other two young men are also students of Presidency College, one reading Bengali and the other History. Poverty sits with assurance on their shoulders, the kind of destitution Esbee had never seen on any of his colleagues when he was at College. Their feelings come from the stomach, their defiance is real, there is no room for armchair socialism.

Esbee recalls his connections with the Communist Party of India (as it then was) and the work he has done for the Students' Federation — the youth arm of the Party. The young men are mollified a little, conversation becomes relaxed, even friendly.

'They blame everything on the students,' the Economist says. 'Anyone who does anything is branded a Naxalite, whipped into jail and then tortured till he gives his friends away. And they hope to kill the Movement this way. But they can't, you see. There are too many of us and we have nothing to lose. If we die by a bullet, serving a cause, it is better than starving to death, and seeing our mothers and sisters and brothers wither away in front of our eyes.'

'Promises are not enough any more,' the Historian cuts in. 'We want jobs, we want food. And we want it now.'

'But how can you get these things if colleges are shut up and ...?'

'What's the good of College, anyway? Look, from this University alone they turn out over thirty thousand graduates every year. But are there jobs for them? Yes, if your brother or your uncle works in

Unilever and you live in New Alipore. Otherwise, no! Even in the advertisements nowadays, they add "Graduates of Calcutta University need not apply". Minimum qualifications for a Grade IV clerk these days is an MA and then you earn eighty rupees [about £4 a month]. And then they say it is all because of the students, if they didn't threaten the professors and walk out of exam halls, there would be no trouble.'

The Economist is doing most of the talking, the other two remain silent. Esbee wants another opinion and he is curious to find out how dictating which questions are to be asked in an exam can be justified. So he turns to the student of Bengali.

'All right,' the young man replies, 'take Nikhil here. He is a student of Economics. He stood fourth in the School Final, out of sixty thousand students. So he is no fool, and he gets a scholarship of sixteen rupees [less than £1] a month. But he has to support his mother and four sisters. So he does six tuitions a week. When one of the girls fell ill, he had to take on more to pay the doctor's bill, because there was no room in the hospital. There is no electricity in the house, and kerosene costs money.'

'Yes, I can understand ...' Esbee begins.

'So,' the boy continues, ignoring the interruption, 'he comes to College to study Economics. If he reads the originals, there are more than a hundred books for the Honours course. He cannot afford to buy any of them, so he goes to the Library. But there is a long queue because most of the other students are in a similar position. So he buys the cheap *Notebooks* which give "predictions" for exam questions. In fact most students do. And who are the authors of these "predictions"? The same professors who teach in the College and University. Why do they write these books? Because their salaries are not enough to support even half a man let alone a whole family. So Nikhil goes into the exam hall, like thousands of others, and if the expected questions (which he has prepared) turn up, then everybody is happy. But if there is a bungle and they don't turn up, what does he do? He knows nothing more about his subject than those specific questions and answers. Does he sit down quietly and fail? It is hard enough *with* a degree, but without it ...?'

There is fire in his eyes, beads of perspiration roll down his cheeks. Esbee keeps guiltily silent.

'Why should we put up with it?' the Historian interjects. 'We *want* to study, we are not stupid. But we are just not allowed to live like human beings. These mother-rapers want it all for themselves.'

'But what about all the murders and bombs and violence?'

'What is murder? What is violence?' Nikhil shouts. 'When my father died of TB, what was that? It can be treated nowadays, you know. But the factory in which he was working gave him the sack because he was too ill. There was no money in the house. So he died.

And then my little sister followed, she was only two. What was that? You tell me *dada*, what was that?'

Chastened into silence, Esbee learnt more that afternoon than in all the years of College. The Naxalite movement had started in Presidency because the brightest minds came to the College. Also, the class origins of the majority of Presidency students had shifted radically towards the lower ends of the socio-economic ladder in the last decade. So, being very poor and bright, the psychic mixture was an explosive one. The specific ideology which motivates actions will be chosen at random, it wouldn't matter which revolutionary handbook you read. You will merely want some of the things you see other people possess. And since you are convinced that you are no less talented than the privileged few, you will be driven by a messianic zeal to destroy the sources of power which perpetuate this merciless and unjust system.

After a month in Calcutta, Esbee was convinced that only the middle class hate the city. The ICI executive, living in a company flat in New Alipore and guzzling scotch at twelve pounds a bottle, feels a little uneasy, but his complaints are not the most vociferous. Because he is above that pathetic income bracket which produces social anaemia under the façade of a pious superiority. The England-returned journalist on eight hundred rupees (about £40) a month is acrid in his denunciations because he is soon going to be out of a job. His false accent imbibed from an English-medium school impresses no one any more.

The insulation of the middle class from all other strata of society has always been more pronounced in Bengal than anywhere else in India. This is the class from which, proverbially, intellectuals, artists, writers and revolutionaries have sprung in times gone by. But whatever revolution may be going on in Calcutta right now is an ad hoc one, not primarily intellectual in character. There are a few leaders but they don't come from the old-type bookish families. All kinds of idiotic anglicizations have been discarded, sexual morality has undergone a change which would not have been thought possible even four or five years ago. The wretched lashes of Queen Victoria's rule have been finally expunged; Calvinism, imported from the early Scots pioneers in imperialism, has been flagrantly discarded.

Life is unsafe, pointillist, defiant of causation. Because a moribund and hypocritical society has been shaken to its foundations. The mala fide equation of age with wisdom is no longer accepted. And to be young in Calcutta today is a rich and rewarding exerience provided you don't come from the class whose existence is threatened.

Of course there are 'liberal' objections to such a state of affairs. But Esbee has some knowledge of the evil and hideous ways in which this present victim class once operated. The average middle-class Bengali is a vermin and a fake *sadhu* in the same body. He asserts total wisdom when his ignorance is fathomless; he instructs you in ethics when what he really wants is the preservation of the status quo and the continued right to remain smugly comfortable. Nowhere in the world are there such feelings of superiority combined with naked obsequiousness, such somnolent lethargy cloaked in *folie de grandeur*, than in this middle-class Bengali.

Esbee came away from Coffee House a wiser man. These young lads were doing what he had never had the guts to do — leading a concerted assault on a senile and decadent society.

Appropriately, the heavens caved in minutes after Esbee walked out of Coffee House. As if by magic the huge heavy drops which had suddenly gathered up there in the sky were now pounding down on the earth below with relentless hysteria. Even the noise of the rain on Calcutta pavements was different from similar sounds he had heard elsewhere. It was the instant, electric transition that made the contrast — a dark, drowsy calm one moment, and the ferocious sound of battering globules all round the very next.

In the small time it took him to race back from the street to the shelter of Coffee House, Esbee was drenched from every hair on his head to the tips of his toe nails. Was Nature working in cahoots with these 'young lads'? Or had the Naxalites alighted upon a singular rhythm, a kind of *mantra*, which would swing in tune with the most common and easily comprehended phenomenon in the old Imperial province of Bengal — the Monsoon?

Two hours later, when Esbee walked down the stone stairs of Coffee House, the cigarette vendor who normally sat at the bottom of the staircase had gone; instead there was a flood of gurgling liquid lapping at the edges of the spittoon. Esbee took off his shoes and rolled up his trousers, not realizing that there was no way he could keep himself dry — when he waded out into the street, the water reached his chest. He understood then why his three young friends had burst into laughter when he had said, 'I see the rain has stopped, and so I must really rush. I have an appointment in half an hour.'

For the spectacle on the street was beyond comparison with anything he had known in his youth in the same city. Several cars were buoyed down on the road, more than half-immersed in the flood; some of the stalls were completely covered over by the water, with sticks of bamboo showing like masts on a sinking ship. There were no trams, buses or taxis — in short there was no form of motorized transport.

The few men who defiantly plodded through the mildly billowing waves of foamy liquid looked like specks of flotsam; the sky seemed frozen in a passive immobility, which was wickedly reflected down below. There was little or no motion anywhere about and a stranger might have imagined some recent plague or famine or perhaps even devastation by a hostile power. He *might* have connected the scene before him with those proverbial agencies of desolation if only he were prevented by some magic from seeing and smelling the yellow, suppurating effluence, which was really no more than a hugely swollen gutter, all round him. The papers next day would not give it more than two column inches in small print.

Of course, a didactic sermon started composing itself in Esbee's mind. The inclination towards instant punditry was hard to resist. In his most ponderous Oxbridge accent, Esbee heard himself intoning, 'Here, in what was once called the Second City of the Empire, a mere two-hour downpour has seized the guts and sinews of one of the principal thoroughfares. No form of transport is available, important appointments cannot be kept. Even walking on foot is hazardous, as the gaping holes on the roads, normally at least visible to the naked eye, are now covered by this opaque, chocolate-coloured liquid, carrying perhaps more germs per unit volume than even that legendary fountain of putrefaction, the Ganges. If there was such a thing as "the drainage system" in this city, the phrase must appear abstruse and incomprehensible to the present inhabitants of the metropolis.'

It was easy and facile to fall into this trap. Members of the World Health Organization (WHO), representatives from myriads of do-gooding institutions all over the globe, had succumbed to the temptation of exploding in outrage and impotent fury at the spectacle of a city which was being allowed, indeed encouraged, to go literally down the drain. But what of the people who lived here? Buffeted on one side by a frenzied and mounting violence and being abandoned to eke out the unproductive agony of their existence on the other, the conspicuous absence of the most elementary amenities of urban living had long been absorbed into the mental landscape of the entire population.

Whenever rain fell, floods would occur, there would be no transport for hours. Electricity would be cut off at least three or four times a day. Telephones would not work. Hospitals would not house the sick. Bombs would explode and people would be shot or knifed to death on the streets. Black-marketeers would hoard food grains and sell them at astronomic prices. Government officials would collude. Bribery would be part of normal experience; if you wanted anything done, you would have to genuflect.

This was the accepted manifesto of daily life, indelibly stamped on the subconscious of the native Calcuttan. It was only the stranger who suffered; the indigenous population had developed a degree of immunity which was yet another astonishing, if perverted, display of the adaptability of the human system.

Walking down College Street, Esbee chanced upon yet another

ingenious exhibition of Bengali versatility. Since there was no motorized transport, and since there were bound to be *babus* (such as Esbee himself) who had cash in their pockets, but who would prefer not to brave the potholes and quagmires of the unseeable streets, rickshaws had sprouted on the street, like acne on an adolescent face.

These two-wheeled contraptions — with a man acting as a beast of burden, pulling at a leash, while the fare sat high above the ground — were the slowest, least used and most humanly degrading mode of transport normally available in Calcutta. (Significantly, they had been banned in all other principal cities in India, but not here in Calcutta, the hometown of Rabindranath Tagore, the poet and philosopher who sang paeons of praise for 'human dignity'.) But with the Monsoon floods, they came uniquely into their own. For neither bicycles nor motorbikes were high enough to rise above the water level of an average two-hour drenching. Ordinary taxis, with their low chassis and drooping engines, suffered the same fate. So did trams and buses, though these were unserviceable because of the condition of the road surface rather than the level of rain-water.

So rickshaws were the only vehicles available. And Esbee, overcoming his initial squeamishness, jumped into one which was being pulled by the healthiest-looking of the scrawny men around.

The rickshaw-puller was twenty-six though he looked at least forty. His face was creased and haggard. The ribs showed on the sides of his chest and around the belly; thin ridges of stretched skin brought out his Adam's apple in sharp relief. He was wearing only a small piece of cloth round his loins. For even with the rain, the temperature was in the mid nineties with the humidity as close as a strangulating fist. The sun lashed at his black, sweat-pouring face, while he panted and puffed his way on bare feet through the water. At the end of the ride, nearly an hour later, when they had arrived in an area of town where the water was only ankle-deep, Esbee asked, 'How much?'

'Oh, sahib,' the rickshaw-puller replied, 'just as it pleases you. I am a poor man, this rickshaw does not belong to me. I have to pay the owner.' When Esbee handed over a five-rupee note (about twenty-five pence of British money) the man burst into sobs and knelt down and touched Esbee's feet in a gesture of homage.

As he climbed the steps of the annexe to rejoin his beloved family, Esbee computed that the man had earned less in a muscle-straining hour than the price of a packet of cigarettes — and even then he had been overwhelmed by our author's apparent generosity.

But such, gentle reader, is the contrary nature of human experience, that into this still pool of philosophic contemplation, without so much as a run-up, Pamela hurled an earth-quaking boulder.

'All these beggars everywhere we go. The children are terrified to walk in the streets. And then the crows, they break plates and leave their droppings all over the place. We would be better off in a tent in the middle of the Sahara than here in the house of your friend "the Prince". Last night I saw a cockroach, a big fat one, right there in the loo. Doesn't even have water, let alone a seat. This is hell! Can't you do something?'

It was a poignant query and one which had plagued Esbee for a long time. Could he do something? If so, what? Could he wave a magic wand and make cockroaches disappear, create seats on loos, burn lethargy out of the Bengali system so that efficiency took the place of procrastination, honour replaced mendacity? Or were these things somehow permanent? For if they were, should the solution not be to seek a more salubrious haven?

The exile is always under attack from both sides. Branded a traitor in the country of his birth, he is treated as an officious nuisance when he starts complaining about conditions in his host country. The same person is called snobbish and superior from one side of the fence, while dismissed as a nincompoop with a chip on his shoulder from the other.

How obscene Pamela's complaints would seem to the young lads in Coffee House, how luxuriously irrelevant they would appear to the rickshaw-puller! Yet how eminently reasonable they sounded to anglicized Esbee. Caught between mutually repulsive fields of force, the Indo-Anglian felt a tide of resentment rising within him. Yet in a very intense way, his wife's carping attitude irritated him even more. How did all this come about? What had the British done round here for over two hundred years?

It was easy to seek refuge in political and historical generalities. But it was far more difficult to deal with the specific at hand. Blaming an Imperial power which had cunningly outmanoeuvred a band of warring natives some centuries ago was no solution to mosquito bites, waterless bathrooms, rainflooded streets and the clawing hands of beggars in the market. If you had to bribe your way to a cinema seat now, it was pointless to pronounce a retrospective reprimand on Macaulay and Curzon in the latter half of the twentieth century.

It was precisely this dialectic of nowhereness that worried him. In an exact sense, Esbee was a man without a country; there was no place he could call his own; no nation or cause to which he could pledge his unswerving loyalty. What little virtue there was in railing against chauvinism was exposed for what it was — sour grapes. Yet if one was to believe in that mystical concept called 'Free Will', then there must have been a time when the options were open ... And Esbee had not started at the bottom of the ladder. So ... what was it? Why was he homeless?

Pendulating between extremes of self-love and egocentric disgust, Esbee was traumatized by Calcutta. In England he would play Devil's Advocate and defend Indians against blanket attacks of parochialism, ghetto mentality, incapacity to adopt British standards etc. In India the precise opposite occurred. Esbee defended the country of his adoption, spurned indigenous criticism and attempted to project the impression that his assimilation of Western mores was total and flawless. Neither of these stances was honest of course. But Esbee was hard put to find a mechanics of social and intellectual behaviour which would be wholly consistent with the demands of his personal psyche and yet remain viable, capable of being understood.

It was not just the infelicities of language, but really those of ethos that intruded continually. He understood! But he could not get himself across for want of that commonly shared shorthand of culture, ritual and subconscious imagery. In this sense he was in perpetual suspension, a medium at home in neither world. A mere go-between.

Strangely, a large part of his alienation resulted from a quasi-Brahminical craving for purity, both physical and intellectual. Esbee hated mess, both in the untidy acquiescence to nebulous doctrine, as well as in the indifference with which physical waste and neglect were institutionalized. In his mind there seemed to be an indissoluble, if not quite easily perceived or provable, link between intellectual decay and physical death. Of course it was a slippery slope, this. Followed to its logical conclusion, it could lead to Hitler via Caligula. Nevertheless, some part of his being insisted that a city's ethos *could* be reflected in its sewage system; that a man's hypocrisy might be the other side of the coin of a powerless and physically disintegrating personality.

Esbee had to admit that his obsession with decay and Death verged on the pathological. But the crucial question was: Did he seek out the evidence? Or was the data already there, ignored by the guardians of healthy bourgeois living, just in case it intruded into the fantasy world of scotch and soda, gold brocaded saris, air conditioned bedrooms and the serene disregard of an external reality which could not be countenanced except in the demented delirium within a padded cell?

Death came in many masks, of course, in this wonderfully colourful and contrasting city: in the putrescent face of waste; in the yellowing pus spurting out of an over-ripe boil; in the decay of youth; in hope mangled to cynical hypocrisy. And soon, very soon, Esbee was to witness such a special Death himself, though the mask it would wear could be given a different name.

'Now, what do you say to another drink?' Arun ventures.

Esbee says yes, the waiter is summoned, two large Black Knights (Indian whisky) are ordered and he leans forward in his seat for the next instalment of the story. Arun is in his early thirties, a bachelor, journalist on an English daily and an acknowledged expert on 'Life'. His hand shakes as he reaches for the glass, bubbles of saliva lodge precariously at the corners of his mouth and his eyes are tinged red. It is only six o'clock in the evening and this bar in Calcutta is fast filling up with the effluence from closed offices.

'When I was in Oxford ...' Arun begins. Esbee waits patiently for this opening-shot ritual to be over, for he has heard the same sentence a dozen times already. 'There is nothing here, nothing. No one ... you know, no one who ...'

'Yes,' Esbee queries, hoping to urge his companion to finish at least one of his statements. 'Really no one,' Arun repeats, swivelling his head from left to right and back again. 'I am the best writer in Calcutta, you know. I mean ... You should see some of their stuff. Unreadable! Totally unreadable! They don't know English! What can you do? Nothing. I mean, we understand each other, you and me, we understand each other, don't we?'

Esbee tries hard to suppress a smile; there are heavy penalties for nosing in from the other side of a one-way street.

'Do you think I could get a job in England? Would you help me please? You must know lots of people, you are a best-selling author, aren't you? And we've been friends, haven't we? All these years, I've always spoken up for you ... you know, I've never let them attack you and get away with it. I always had faith in you, I knew you would make it some day, no matter what they said.'

Whisky-tears flood down Arun's face, jerky sobs ejaculate from his throat, a despairing palm clutches Esbee's hand. 'I want to get out of here. This place is hell, really, you can't imagine how bad it is. It's a kind of nightmare. I want to talk to you about it, really. How can I get out? Do you think they will accept me in England?'

Esbee wants to say yes and no. People were accepted in England, yes, even brown-skinned *babus*. Not everyone sympathized with Enoch Powell, there weren't dockers in every pub. Overt discrimination was rare, especially towards an educated young man. And yet there was a certain something, an indefinable air of hostility, difficult to pinpoint, elusive because one was never sure how much came from within oneself and how much from the outside. It was ambiguous. Polite unspoken aversion to foreigners was endemic in the English character — whatever the colour of the intruder. It only erupted into riots and marches when the dichotomy was sharpened in an economically deprived context. A good writer would never be castigated merely because he was black or brown; no publisher would turn him down because of his race or creed. But he might be patronized, and sometimes the latter response might be harder to stomach. Esbee wants to explain, if only to clarify ideas in his own mind by attempting to put them across. But he is not given the chance.

Arun bangs his fists on the table, gurgling words which merge into each other. He lurches forward from one table to another as he wends his way to the loo. Esbee asks the waiter for the bill and pays for the full session of five rounds. Arun returns to the table, swills down the remnants of his whisky and asks for another one. The waiter looks enquiringly; helplessly Esbee nods a yes. Talk continues, circular, obsessive and in violent defiance of grammar, diction and audibility. Finally, the two of them rise and emerge into the sticky heat of a monsoon evening in Calcutta. Esbee puts his friend into a taxi and re-enters the air-conditioned bar for a quiet, expensive scotch all by himself.

Three days later Esbee meets Arun again, sober this time, in his office at eleven in the morning. He is an Assistant Editor on the paper and shares the room with a colleague. After the initial exchanges of introductions, conversation begins. 'As a writer, don't you feel you have an obligation towards your country, to the place where you were born and the people who brought you up?'

Esbee's short answer is no.

Undaunted, Arun launches into a diatribe. 'How can you turn your back to all that is going on in India? It may be materially more rewarding for you in England but they will never accept you. Even when you've lived there for twenty years, you'll still remain a second-class citizen. This is your country after all. Don't you feel you ought to contribute something towards its reconstruction and development? India needs people like you. If you just say goodbye, what hope is there? You mustn't only think of yourself, you must be less selfish in your attitude towards your motherland.'

Esbee replies he is not a missionary and the altruistic urge has never been a marked feature of his personality. Esbee is a writer and his ideas of what a writer ought to do simply do not coincide with those of his learned friend. Sorry!

'But really, don't you see what is going on in India, even here in Calcutta, is tremendously exciting? An ancient culture, with traditions and values dating back some three thousand years and more, is being built anew. For a writer this is the most exciting place in the world, especially if he has been lucky enough to have been born an Indian. Don't you see that?'

Esbee replies that he had often heard avant garde students of 'creative writing' at American universities and believers in transcendental consciousness say so. And perhaps it is. For them, not him.

'Then what is the purpose of writing? I haven't read any of your books but I have seen the reviews. And I think up to now you have been writing mostly about yourself, haven't you. But what will you do now? You should really concern yourself with something serious.'

Very humbly, Esbee replies that he was under the impression that he had been deadly serious all along. One doesn't do without food, clothes and shelter for years and put down a million words on paper just to prove how flippant one is.

'Yes,' says the guru, 'but you really should think deeply about it. You simply can't turn your back on the past and your heritage. It's all very well to go West and all that. But you must remember that even Madhusudan Dutt had to come back and Sri Aurobindo ...'

'I am simply not in that class,' Esbee cuts in, 'so the problem doesn't arise.'

Arun looks deeply and steadily at Esbee. The colleague's face carries marked signs of disapproval. Esbee feels it is time for him to leave. 'We must have another drink sometime,' he offers as a parting shot. 'I enjoyed our last session very much.'

'Yes, yes,' Arun replies, not picking up the cue.

As he walks out of the room and down the corridor, Esbee reflects upon the marvel of human memory. If one remembered every single word one had ever spoken, how utterly unbearable life would be.

4

Journey into Carnage

They call me master because of some
magic in my speech and thoughts; but I
am a frightened child in the presence
of Death.

MAURICE MAETERLINCK, *Death*

We must not fear death. This would be
paying it too much honour ... Death
could not be too far demoted from the
sacred status normally attributed to it.
Nothing is more despicable than respect
based on fear. And from this point of
view, death is no more worthy of respect
than Nero or the inspector at my local
police station.

ALBERT CAMUS, *Carnets*

This chapter owes its inception to the *Sunday Times* (London). As I
was going to Calcutta — at my own expense — to visit my dying
mother, I requested the paper to commission a piece by me on
Bangladesh. I fancied I had some 'special' qualifications for the job
which their staff writers — however brilliant and professional —
lacked. I spoke Bengali, understood the East Bengali dialect and my
close relations still lived in Barisal (the second largest town in what
was then East Pakistan). I myself had visited that part of the world
several times when I was young. And I felt, perhaps with a
characteristic, un-English lack of modesty, that my command of
English was somewhat superior to that of local Asiatic reporters who
seconded for British papers.

My pleas were favourably received and on the evening before I left
London (8th July, 1971), I was handed a letter signed by the editor of
the paper, declaring that I was on an unspecified mission on behalf of
the *Sunday Times*. On my return to London some eight weeks later, I
realized that during my mission in East Pakistan I had chanced upon
information which was potential political dynamite. The

nformation was simply this: India was directly involved in the insurgent movements in East Pakistan; the Mukti Bahini was a eunuch front, an image sedulously fostered by the Indian Government to camouflage its own extensive guerilla activities within the boundaries of another nation.

At the time, however, India was loudly proclaiming, in the UN and other international forums, that she was playing no part whatsoever in what was going on inside East Pakistan, that her hands were clean, and that her sole concern was the innocent non-military one of repatriation of the millions of refugees who had poured in through the border into her territory.

Whatever the morality of the case (and I personally wholly approved of intervention, either by India, the UN or any other power), India's international stance and pious posturings were clearly in defiance of the facts as I had witnessed them. And no journalist, either Western or Eastern, had written to say this — perhaps because some didn't know and others were gagged or willingly colluded. The degree of India's wrath against me personally, when the whole story was finally published, might be gauged from the fact that friends and relations of mine in Calcutta, Bombay and Delhi, were severely interrogated by the CID and placed under surveillance. I was branded a dangerous subversive and blacklisted at the Indian High Commission in London.

So I set to writing the story and presented it to the paper some four days later. After a few preliminary skirmishes and the third rewrite, it was turned down. Quite simply because I was not believed.

So I walked two floors down and offered it to the *Guardian*. A week later it was published under the title 'Big Brother Goes to War' without a word of alteration. A minor diplomatic contretemps did take place and I received a few threatening telephone calls. I was cast in the role of Judas when the 'Pakistan Solidarity Front,' in an open letter to Mr Edward Heath on the eve of Mrs Gandhi's visit to London, used my article to support the brutal genocide in Bangladesh. As it happened, my story was amply substantiated exactly three months later by the words and deeds of the Indian Government itself.

A small but significant episode connected me personally with my mission in Bangladesh. The day after I reached Calcutta, I was told that my aunt, who lived in Barisal, had just arrived from there, along with her two grown-up daughters. My uncle — a seventy-five year-old *zamindar* (landowner) who had lived all his life in East Pakistan — had been taken away by the Pakistan Army and presumably shot or dumped in a cell to die.

He was a stubborn man and had gone to his death with a naive cry of faith on his lips — 'What have I done?' Twice before in the last twenty-five years, when anti-Hindu persecution in East Pakistan had reached inconsolable proportions, large numbers of Hindus had migrated to West Bengal (India) to escape massacre. Each time such an exodus took place, my uncle scoffed at 'these spineless cowards, leaving the land of their fathers.' An innocent man never suffers, the Muslims are human, they have been exploited too long, those they rise up against deserve their wrath. 'My *prajas* [subjects, tenants] love me, I have been a father to them, I have never snatched rice from the mouths of their infants — like some people have. They will never turn against me, I love them like my own children.'

He was right of course. His *prajas* never did turn against him. When the West Pak Army was about to swoop down on his farm, two of his faithful Muslim 'children' had even come over to warn him, risking their own lives. They advised that he should go away, hide for a few days and then sneak out of the country. But he had dismissed their pleas with aristocratic hauteur: 'This is my land, this is where I was born. My father lived here, and his father before him. I shall not leave my *paitreyik vite* [father's land], they will have to kill me first, and they will never dare do that. I am a Chakravarti, I shall not dishonour the name of my ancestors.'

The men who took him away were not his *prajas*. They wore military uniform, prodded him along with bayonets and came from a land some 1,200 miles away. Racially, they were as different from those he loved 'like my own children' as an Irish Catholic is from a Sicilian peasant. Of course it is indecent to romanticize death, but I can't help feeling a horrified fascination for his kind of old-fashioned faith in humanity. And I would have loved to know the words he spoke the moment before they put an end to his simple seventy-five-year-old life.

The surviving female members of the family had hidden in nearby marshland, more to protect their 'honour' than their lives. When night fell, they had gathered a bagful of clothes, some food and a few trinkets of jewellery, and bidden farewell to the old ancestral house. On leaving the land of their fathers, all three women had prostrated themselves on the ground and prayed to the family God to protect their 'man'.

It was an ill-fated prayer and none of them carried any hope in her heart. They knew that the journey ahead would be long and gruelling, perhaps they themselves would die in the hands of a soldier. Or worse! It was some eighty miles to the border of India, the old woman was sixty-seven and suffered from gout, there were spies and *razakars* (turncoats) all along the way. The stories they had heard were not comforting, nor was the torrential monsoon shower which pasted their saris to the skin.

When they finally arrived in Calcutta, they could not even cry. The mother lay on the bed, staring up at the ceiling, without a flicker of recognition in her eyes. Her two daughters sat at her feet, motionless as dummies. For two whole days they had to be force-fed on liquid glucose. Every time a doctor went near the feverish old woman, she jerked away as if she had been stung by an adder. The younger women talked, but the words were disconnected, frenzied. 'Must not go in the light. Water ... Home fried potatoes. Don't eat them all up. They'll see us. No, no, we shall die first than ...'

They had practised the same drill, a thousand times over, during their ten-day journey to Calcutta. The mother would tie a sari round the necks of both her daughters, then they would climb a tree with a sturdy branch high enough above the ground. Then they would tie the other end of the sari to the branch, ready to swing at the sound of a rifle shot or the grinding of military tanks. The mother would remain on the ground, supervising operations. 'The beasts' would not want to rape a sixty-seven-year-old woman. No feature in this unique tableau was the creation of an original or psychotic mind. During their eighty-mile trek, all three travellers had witnessed hundreds (literally) of women, even girls in their early teens, dangling from trees, open-eyed death staring out of their faces. Such was their commitment to Hindu 'honour' against Muslim rape, such their total despair.

Nor was this the end of the story. For ten days and ten nights they had waded through marsh and swamp, rice fields and streams. At daybreak each day they had sought refuge in a pond or a river, sea-weeds and water plants covering them over. Gun boats had passed them on the wide rivers, corpses had floated by grazing their skins. The old woman had caught fever on the third day of their journey but she had plodded on. Her daughters acted on her instructions as if they were automatons. One time they had clung to the bottom of a dinghy at night to get them further ahead — 'Dare not ask for help in case ...' Twice the young girls were propositioned by men on the same trail, Hindus, wanting a bit of spare on the free. The mother had whipped them off with true-blue Chakravarti regality. 'You curs,' she had shouted, 'get away from my daughters. Or else you'll pay for your misdeeds.' The misdoers had vanished, the *razakars* had been avoided, the Army men hoodwinked. A mother and her two daughters had reached the border with an 'honourable' discharge. The Family God was praised, and then all three fell into a swoon from which they took a long time to recover. When they arrived in Calcutta, none of them could even cry. Or speak.

I call this a *small* episode because seen through the daunting binoculars from 'Objectivity & Co.', what happened was minor, perhaps even irrelevant to 'the larger issues at stake here, the millions of lives being held to ransom, the indiscriminate violation of human dignity etc.' My uncle was an old man, he would have died anway sooner rather than later. And as for the three women who made that hazardous journey, well, people had done far more for far greater causes than the mere saving of their 'honours' — wherever that commodity might come from. In numerical terms, they were a myopic minority; in terms of human suffering, well, it was a sad thing for those three, but there wasn't a newspaper story there at all. It had happened to millions of other people all over the world; is still happening as a matter of fact. Nothing unique, actually.

Quite true! But that episode was perhaps a true description of twentieth-century man, faced in real life with spectacles he sees on the goggle-box every night, to which he has become inured: sheer terror and the knowledge that he is just an animal in the face of it.

If I die tomorrow, will I be a mere number among others, or will my wife be weeping for me? It is a childishly self-centred question, I know, but I think it is more important than the diarrhoeal flood of journalese that conscientious editors and their subs release on us every day. The fact that I am alive cannot be computed. And I shouldn't think that too many editors — if they have a toothache or a potential divorce on their hands or are about to launch into an alcoholic binge with their mistress or their colleague — feel differently either. But they go on acting as if they do. And the game goes on. Reality is bandaged up, the cascading flow of blood is stopped by judicious application of antiseptic, statistics insulate, and the pure holy air of nonchalant indifference is fanned in once again.

It is possible of course that the people who do these jobs have to inoculate themselves against personal involvement or else they'd land up in a loony bin. The hangman cannot afford to have a love affair with the woman in the condemned cell; the doctor in charge of cancer ward should not, professionally, identify too closely with his patients; the reporter ... But this is where the whole hideous lie is germinated. There are certain correct ways of applying anaesthetic; these methods are sacrosanct, they have stood the test of time etc. And no one dares defy them. Because if anyone does, the punishment is simple excommunication, *ex cathedra* judgement without appeal. But to surrender abjectly is to court an even worse fate — for only in challenge do we really live.

The most gruesome act of genocide and human atrocity in recorded history took place in Bangladesh between 25th March and 31st December of 1971. In that short time, three million people were killed, ten million terrorized out of their homes, and two hundred thousand women were systematically raped every day for several months by groups of soldiers in army barracks. These figures by themselves do not make the adequate emotional impact, there is no automatic quantum jump in the degree of horror we feel when 'three hundred thousand' (bodies) is multiplied by ten to raise it to 'three million'. There is no proportional increase in sorrow in the heart of a soldier when he sees five hundred men lying dead on a battlefield from when a comrade-in-arms falls by his side; it is as difficult to conceive of fourteen light years as of forty-four. The human mind can visualize misfortune in the concrete and react with grief only up to a certain point. After that the responsive mechanism switches off to prevent blowing a fuse from over-loading, and abstractions take over. Of course the degree of alienation must increase as we get more and more frequently bombarded with stories and pictures of human misery. For sheer survival we must construct a fantasy world in which 'it could never happen here'. The reality in Ulster is distanced by the TV screen, the horror in Vietnam was disenfranchised by repeated visual exposure to the mechanics of war. Till there comes a time when feeling is impossible, only a vague intellectual repugnance continues to irritate the sensitive conscience.

But the figures still do serve a purpose, if only by comparison. The first ever time Londoners were really jolted into concern over Ulster was when a bomb went off in the Post Office Tower. Although no one was killed, the media devoted more time and attention to that single incident than to the ten other explosions and three deaths that took place in Northern Ireland on the same day. The ratio is worth noting, for talking of the *most* gruesome massacre in recorded history, Adolf Hitler immediately springs to mind.

Six million Jews *were* incinerated in gas ovens — twice the Bangladesh figure. But the Fuehrer's activities were nowhere near as publicized at the time they were happening, and he took ten long years to perpetrate that heinous genocide. The West Pak Army decimated an entire community in less than nine months and the whole world knew of this while it was going on. I do not believe that anything like it could have happened in the Western world without one or other of the major powers rushing in to prevent it, allowing even for the enormous attendant risks. Hungary, Czechoslovakia, Suez, Poland, South Africa or even the Congo or Biafra horrors, do not begin to match the scale on which the Bangladesh slaughters took place. Yet no nation, least of all India, did anything about it. When and if all the facts are known, historians will appraise the role played by the land of Nehru and Gandhi in this sordid affair. But it is my belief that India was a party to the massacre, even if only by omission, and her subsequent actions were prompted more by self-interest than humane concern for the lives of innocent men and women.

It is important to bear these 'facts' in mind, for when I went on my expedition to Bangladesh, I did not know them. I was aware that some hideous tragedy was taking place, and the story of my aunt and her two daughters spurred me to 'do something about it'. But I had no idea of the incredible dimensions of the horror, nor could I really 'feel' what it must be like to have experienced the savage pain of those to whom these things had happened.

In Calcutta I saw and heard a great deal which sickened and disgusted me. The Chief Co-ordinator for Refugee Relief and Rehabilitation, sitting in his air-conditioned office, with two aides-de-camp and three messenger boys, talking of 'the dire need to teach these people the efficacy of self-help'; the daughter of one of the wealthiest industrialists in India, freshly back from New York, expostulating on 'the people's war' and her once-weekly jaunts in an army jeep to deliver supplies 'to the valiant fighters who are heroically carrying on the struggle for liberation'; the journalist in a three-piece gabardine suit (in the middle of a Calcutta summer), drawing in cigarette smoke through a six-inch long holder and writing leaders about the plight of refugees in the camps, and jocularly confessing that there was no need to go and see for himself as he had looked at the photographs — 'I can just *imagine* how ghastly it must be for those wretched creatures.'

But the thing that angered me most was the behaviour of those who were directly involved with the fate of that ravaged nation at the time. For I believed that this was a situation in which a writer could actually 'do' something. If the full extent of the tragedy were widely publicized and hammered home in powerful prose, even the most recalcitrant government would be forced to take notice, public opinion would be aroused (I mean in the West, of course) and intervention would take place before floods of blood and grief were unleashed once again. Perhaps I was over-optimistic about politicians; perhaps I exaggerated the powers of the pen, the changes a writer can bring about. But it was worth a try, as writers have always believed.

The Secretary General of the Border Security Forces — an urbane Indian gentleman who read Rilke in German and had taken a degree from one of the Oxbridge colleges — was orientally obstructive at first, and then downright threatening. If I persisted in my efforts to get into East Pakistan I would be arrested; he would be left with no option. So I assured him I would not go against his instructions, certainly not without obtaining his permission beforehand — especially as he had been so obliging and spoken with me for all of five minutes.

Then I approached the exiled representatives of the people of East Pakistan. And for sheer discourtesy, the officials in the Bangladesh mission in Calcutta could not be excelled. I met the erstwhile Deputy High Commissioner of Pakistan (who had reneged on Yahya Khan and avowed his loyalty to Sheikh Mujib), and after a short interview conducted under the most regal formalities, he handed me over to his PR. From that point on my lessons in humiliation and insult began. For two whole weeks I was kept waiting in the gate-keeper's lodge (the Bangladesh Mission was a quasi-palatial establishment) for four to six hours a day, before the PR granted me a routine two-minute audience with, 'I will try to arrange something for you tomorrow. I very busy just now at this moment to meet Mr. ... from *News of the World* in England, at the Grand Hotel.' Next day I would be lucky to see him at two in the afternoon, if at all. And the same story would be repeated with minor variations on the theme. I put up with it for a fortnight and then resolved to have a go all by myself.

It is worth recording here that during the three weeks I spent in Calcutta, futilely trying to get official approval and help to go inside East Pakistan, twice-weekly soirées were organized by the Bangladesh Mission with the co-operation of the Border Security Forces (Indian) for journalists, both foreign and indigenous. But no one who spoke and understood Bengali, and who was not also on the staff of an Indian paper was ever allowed in. Those who were free (the Western journalists) to write what they saw and *heard* had to depend upon an official interpreter; those who did not need a linguistic mediator (Indian journalists) were dependent upon their papers and the bosses who dictated the House policies. As far as I know, I was the only writer who sought and was refused official permisson to enter East Pakistan and see for myself, who spoke and understood Bengali, but who could not be gagged by an Indian agency, as I held a British passport and my credentials had been supplied by a Western newspaper.

Because of this, I believe, grotesque lies were propagated as Biblical truths, inadvertently on one side (Western journalists) and venally on the other (the Indian journalists). For what has happened in Bangladesh is a double tragedy. Millions of men and women have lost their lives. And a large nation has acquired a smaller, potentially rich satellite, while making hypocritical overtures towards concepts of independence and self-determination. I hope I am wrong in my analysis, but I fear that events will go the other way. Already the sky rumbles with the sound of distant thunders, the earth quivers. The explosion is not far away.*

'The big operations are always done by the Indians. I was in that group which blew up those bunkers and opened up the road from Akhaura. And I wasn't allowed to cross the border. We are like a little boy with big brother holding us by the hand. Being on foreign soil, we are quite helpless. We have to do what they tell us. Even our leaders, Makhan bhai and Rab bhai, are wholly in their power.'

The young man who said this to me was a volunteer in the Mukti Fauj, one of some two hundred potential liberation fighters in

*This was written in 1973 and it is appalling to see that my most dire prophecies were fulfilled in the massacre of Sheikh Mujib and his entire family on the morning of 15th August, 1975. The following pages draw upon material first published in my article 'Big Brother Goes to War' (*The Guardian*, 18th September, 1971).

Agartala (on the Indian side of the eastern border of what is now Bangladesh) whose patience was running out. And he was one of the lucky few! At least he had taken part, however peripherally, in a commando raid. Most of his friends had been hanging around for months, waiting for that call-up which never comes.

'Some of us have gone in and thrown a few hand-made grenades. But when it comes to blowing up a bridge or derailing a train, the Indians do it all themselves, taking us along as guides. And then they call it a Mukti Fauj* 'victory'. It isn't that we are ungrateful. But it is our war and our land, we want to do it ourselves.'

This kind of disaffection was pervasive among all the volunteers I spoke to in Agartala. They were being kept out of the action, their leaders had become easy pawns in the hands of the Indian Army and Border Security Forces. They spoke to me about their frustrations because I was not attached to any Indian paper and because I could follow their dialect.

I wanted to get into East Pakistan and see for myself, and Agartala was the best stepping-off point. But getting even there was a problem. The town was a restricted area, foreign nationals and Western correspondents were not allowed in without special permission from New Delhi. When such permission was granted, it was always for a specific purpose like 'inspecting refugee camps', and never extended to more than a day. And even during that time the journalist was not allowed to move around freely. The man in charge of the press information bureau in Agartala told me the story of an American reporter who fretted at having a tail put on him and spent his whole time trying to shake him off, unsuccessfully.

So I had to conceal the fact that I held a British passport. And even though I looked Indian, I was hauled in for questioning at the police station within hours of my landing in Agartala. This was repeated twice afterwards, during my four-day stay; on the last occasion the interrogation lasted for nearly five hours, supervised by an Indian Army officer.

Over the two days I spent in Agartala while trying to get help, I met and talked with some thirty volunteers, sometimes singly, mostly in groups. And it became clear from what they said that neither the officers of the Mukti Fauj nor their de facto superiors would help me cross the border, much less take me along with them on one of their raids. I was an awkward customer.

But by the time they had finally turned me down, I began to get a picture of what was going on. A senior officer in the Indian Air Force, who is related to me, had said in Calcutta, 'See you inside if ever you get there'. I had taken it as a joke at the time. But having spoken to

*Bengali: 'Liberation Army'.

refugees who had just come across and seen a few things myself, the joke didn't seem too funny any more. Chittagong had been bombed; one College lecturer, a refugee from the town, said he had seen two parachutes landing in a field, not far from Fenny. At Agartala airport, I had seen some twelve Indian Air Force planes; two with four propellers and massive bellies and half a dozen tiny single-engined efforts. In addition to these, there were hordes of Dakotas flying in and out every ten minutes, transporting refugees out of the town to various rehabilitation centres.

So I gave up hope of any co-operation from the authorities and decided to go it alone.

Abdul was twenty-four, married with two children, a cycle-rickshaw puller from Comilla in East Pakistan. He was a Muslim and had assumed I was too from my appearance. In Agartala there were not at the time many Hindus who would hire him for two whole days running, as I did, without an urgent reason. While I was haggling with the Mukti Fauj officials, Abdul had ferried me round the town without a murmur.

When repeated promises were followed by recurrent refusals and I was gripped with total exasperation, he suggested we might be able to do it together, just he and I. The idea terrified and lured me. 'How much?' I asked.

'Oh, sahib,' he replied, demurely expressing disgust with himself. *ek sow rupaya* [one hundred rupees].' I smiled, There was a certain irony in his choice. My advance commission from the *Sunday Times* was one hundred pounds: pound to a rupee, my life to his — seemed a fair exchange. So I accepted, calling on defiance, cussedness and all those other honourable assets with which journalists are endowed.

I was aware that there was a two-pronged danger. If I was discovered by the West Pak Army or any of their *razakar* agents, there would be no time for a question and answer session. I would be shot or hanged or tied up and thrown into a river, without even the semblance of a trial. On the other hand, if I was to encounter Mukti Fauj commandos (the goodies) on a raid, and was unable to produce the requisite password, they would hardly stop by for a chat about Marlowe and the latest communication I may have received from the Editor of the *Sunday Times*. They had bullets galore and very little time — I would be summarily despatched.

So when I decided to go into East Pakistan with Abdul, without any official protection, I was behaving like a pig-headed child. I had taken one hundred pounds from a newspaper and I was damn well going to give them their money's worth. And if all those others were coming in my way, well, they'd just have to go to hell. I really couldn't care.

I wish I could say I did what I did from nobler motives. The fact is I didn't. I resented and hated those Bangladesh officials who had treated me like dirt. I was outraged, ashamed of the colour of my skin. Driven to frenzy by a renewed awareness that a Bengali will arse-lick any white-skinned bum! 'I very busy, go to Grand Hotel to meet Mr. ...', I felt low, cheap and mean. And in this battle between self-hate and self-assertion, ego won. I would show them! Even if I was the only one, even if I was feeling scared as hell; *I would go in and come out.* I would dare! I knew I might die in the doing. But I did not let the thought mature in my mind, fielding it with the rationalization, in which I did not sincerely believe, that it would be worth while.

Abdul was not a particularly easy lad to get on with. He did not drink, spoke in tight clipped sentences and never laughed. But there was a controlled passion in his voice, a seething anger which erupted in the most flaming language whenever 'these Punjabi beasts' were mentioned. At first I took this to be an index of political consciousness, the violent reaction of a man who could not acquiesce in the rape of his country, when a small distant power ruled and exploited a larger, weaker and richer nation. But no, he couldn't care less who ruled East Pakistan. They were all the same when they sat in the big chair. No, that was not his gripe. He did not mind if the Awami Leaguers were dumped into the sea; he had not voted in the last elections which preceded the troubles. He had no time for politicians and trouble-makers.

His concern was smaller and his passion more intense than any I have seen in 'professional' revolutionaries on TV. When we talked about *his* land — *aamar zamin* — his eyes glowed, his voice dropped a pitch, assuming the cutting edge of an executioner's sword. The small plot of land (perhaps not much larger than an English country garden) which he owned near Comilla was *his*, it had been given him by his father, it was his legacy, his *paitreyik vite*. All his life he had tended it as his most precious possession. The rice his family ate came out of that land, and so did the potatoes and cauliflowers and onions. Cycle-rickshaw pulling was a supplementary occupation; the reality of his life grew sturdily out of the earth. Now, this vital emblem of his manhood, his very sense of self, had been taken from him. And it was this deprivation that fired the killer's hate in his eyes, the will to avenge spilling over into manic fury.

As an urban animal, living in a mobile technological society, I found it hard to comprehend. I felt an intruder, while he implored my wiser counsel. He said he was 'like a man without half his body'. I noted his words but they did not ring quite true. Not in my ears, not at the time. Later, I snatched a glimpse of what he must have meant, the sense of home, being there, rooted. Words get lost of course, and so does empathy. It is not easy to describe smell and touch and feeling. The *earth* holds you in an invisible mesh. And the moment you leave it, you know you have broken the magic spell which gave meaning and direction and being: the feeling of wet clay squelching about your ankles as you plod through a paddy field; the odour of fresh dung on the thin long ridges of dry mud that separate one crop from another; the stacks of hay that blaze and gold in the roasting sun — indescribable sensory experiences, plucking elemental chords, defying translation.

I did not know what Abdul meant, but I could feel he was arching towards a haven I had never known. Hours of a night later, with the sun yawning under an eastern sky, as we stood in a dirt road in Chok Bazar (on the outskirts of Comilla, within East Pakistan) Abdul pointed to a silver line on the horizon. *'Aiyee aamar zamin'*, he muttered. At that moment I was totally estranged. We had ploughed the night together, sharing danger, coming closer. But just then, when the glob of gold plopped out of the sky, and I was shaking at the knees lest some friendly *razakar* should decide to put us out of our miseries before anything more drastic happened, all Abdul could do was clench his fist. No tears, no sobs jerking out of his throat: just *zamin* — earth. The kind of home that trees have when they send deep and spreading roots under the ground. I knew then that Abdul would never have left his land if he had been a little older. He would have preferred to die rather than let 'these Punjabi beasts' take over — just as my uncle had done. Hindu, Muslim, there was no difference: one umbilical cord, the sinews of the soil holding the peasant soul together.

What then had finally compelled him to abandon the land he loved so dearly?

'Well,' Abdul replied, 'at first they only rounded up the Hindus, burnt their houses and shops, looted their rice, set fire to the haystacks. Some got shot, others fled. Those of us Muslims who had no political associations, the military left alone.

'Then about two months ago, they started handing out arms to these *goondas* who were let out from jail (the euphemistic name for these former jail-birds is *razakar*) and paid them three rupees a day. And these thugs began to loot and shoot whoever and whenever they liked. We had a horrid time, seeing these law-breakers turned law-keepers swaggering through the village, having to keep our tempers in control, giving them whatever they wanted, and hiding for our lives. But even then I did not think of leaving; I would have put up with it a lot longer. I was sure it would all come to an end, Allah would see to that. These thugs would not be there always, and they were not going to drive me out of my own land.

'But later it was even worse. Two days before I came away from Comilla, the Mukti Fauj blew up a small bridge. Then the military drove into our village in a jeep and started firing many, many bullets with their machine gun. They did not pick anyone in particular, they did not ask any questions. Only on the loudspeaker they said this would happen every time any mischief was done in or near our village. If anyone was keeping a mischief-maker in his house or giving food to these trouble-makers, the jeep would return and bullets would pour down. And just before they left the guns went off once again. My hut was riddled with holes, but we escaped being killed. A neighbour's wife died.'

Abdul must have re-lived the scene many times in his mind, till the shock and horror of the original experience had ossified into bitterness and rage. For his voice did not shake as he told the story, the only change was in his eyes — they shone with murderous venom.

'You cannot go on living that way, like a hunted animal, not knowing what will happen next day, in the next hour. I had my wife and children. If I were alone ...'

Yet Abdul had returned to the village twice since that shooting incident. 'Why?' I asked.

'I went back to collect a few of my possessions. I told the neighbours I was taking the wife and children to the in-laws for a few days. It is hard to know whom to trust these days. But now there is no chance for me to go back till all this is over. I have been away too long, they will know I have gone across. And the *razakars* would kill me if they saw me around.'

One final query remained in my mind. Why had he agreed to undertake this hazardous journey with me, especially as he had been a first-hand witness to the brutality of 'these Punjabi beasts'? Couldn't have been just the money? Or could it?

'Oh, Sahib,' Abdul answered, 'we are poor people, we have only our land. It is like our father, mother, wife and children, everything. Without the land, we move about like flies, buzzing and droning, with nowhere to rest. The 'beasts' have driven me away from my land and Allah will punish them for their wickedness. I have done no wrong, and my land will come back to me, one day. I know, I know in my heart. But I am not a learned man, I cannot write in newspapers. So if I can do something, if I can help you to write and make this horrible time end, then I will think I am lucky to be able to do it. I would not ask for money, sahib, but I have to pay rent for my rickshaw and buy food for four of us.'

'I understand,' I said, and pressed the money into his hand. From the look on his face, I knew he would rather not have taken it. His was a symbolic act, mine on the other hand ...?

There were a few simple preparations to be made before we began our journey. I already *looked* like a Muslim: short triangular beard, cropped hair and a three-week growth on the rest of my face, matched my image. By now I had mastered the lingo sufficiently not to be caught out as a rank outsider. And should the eventuality arise, I consoled myself with the thought that I possessed the requisite genital qualification that distinguishes a Muslim from a Hindu. Also, I had learnt the first three verses of the Koran in Urdu by heart, in case instant identification was demanded.

Abdul lent me one of his dirty *lungis* (a long piece of cloth, a little over a yard in width, simply wrapped round the waist) and a vest; I picked up a pair of second-hand sandals in the bazaar. And so, each with a bundle under our arms to show we were travelling, the two of us set off. I tucked the *Sunday Times* letter in the waist band of my *lungi*, more as a good luck talisman than an instrument of defence. For if the crunch came, there would be little time to show my credentials — death would come swiftly in Bangladesh, a hand grenade at my feet, the quick jab of a bayonet in my heart, and, period.

Of course we would take all possible precautions. And Abdul knew the route from past experience. We would avoid the obvious trap at the border, only two miles from Agartala. At the outbreak of the troubles, streams of refugees had poured into India at this point; journalists had gone in and out with equanimity. But now it was heavily patrolled on both sides, there was no civilian traffic either way. Artillery fire was exchanged between the two sides as a matter of routine: I had heard the blasting sounds of gunpowder throughout both the previous two nights I had spent in Agartala.

At first it was a mere speck on the screen, remote, inaudible, harmless. If you *knew* for certain you were going to die, you would never do it, not volitionally, not if you were sane. The possibility exists, but you dismiss it from your mind. You say to yourself you'll come out the winner, you refuse to let the idea take concrete shape: a real bayonet held by a real man, two feet away from you. No, you don't visualize a scene like that, not at the start. It would never happen, not to you. You do think of the aftermath, the glory, the rich satisfaction of having dared, the courage with which you went through it all. But the actual experience, if it were to come, is shrouded in a veil of unthought, as if you could press a button which would catapult you from the beginning to the end, without the dreadful middle forcing itself in tangible, threatening forms.

Then after the beginning, there is silence, an untalkative companion, a slushy field and fireflies blinking in the dark. That is when you start to think, images flash through your mind, that small speck picks up speed, begins to drone a little, somewhat larger, a little less harmless. You entertain yourself with the pleasing thought that 'It is all in the mind'.

A while later, you surrender to the consolations of philosophy for the first time in fifteen years. 'What am I doing this for? What do I hope to prove? Who cares if I live or die? What is the purpose of life? Of human experience? Silly way to come to the end of the road, isn't it? Is death really the end? How do I know there isn't an afterlife? What if God exists after all? What would He look like, I wonder? How firm are my beliefs if they can be knocked about by a stupid little expedition like this? Does one really see the whole of one's past life "spread out on a screen" minutes before the final curtain?' Then suddenly you are whipped back to reality and have your first taste of fear.

A man was squatting on the ground, performing his evacuations. We had come upon him suddenly. The light of the kerosene lamp in front of him had been screened off by tall weeds. As soon as he saw us, the man sprang to his feet, holding a stick in his right hand.

'Shalaam Alikum,' Abdul said, in a quiet unflustered voice.

I started shivering.

The man lowered his stick a little, lifted the kerosene lamp with his left hand and gave us the once over under the flickering light.

'Shalaam Alikum,' he murmured. Then there was a pause, the world heaved in my heart, and finally, where were we going?

'Bibir Bazar,*' Abdul replied, while I fought with a frenetic desire to run.

'Bibir Bazar?' the man repeated, questioning.

'Ha ji [yes Sir]', we both answered.

He looked at Abdul, then at me. The shadows danced; lurking behind his left hand the face looked menacing. It couldn't have lasted more than a couple of minutes, that inquiring silence, but it seemed like an aeon to me. But we did finally pass the test. 'Troubles round here,' the man said. 'It is late.' Would we care to come and rest in his hut for the night?

Not really, Abdul replied, it wasn't far, we would make it in another half hour or so, we were not strangers in these parts. 'Shalaam Alikum.'

'Shalaam Alikum,' our kindly interlocutor answered, as he started to walk away from us.

I inhaled the largest dose of fresh air ever and jogged my feet out of the frame in which they had been frozen. The first one is the toughest, I thought to myself, as I turned to see the light of the kerosene lamp eclipsed by trees and a long stretch of field; won't be as bad as this the next time round. But it was poor consolation. My knees shook, my hands were ice cold and I asked Abdul if we shouldn't turn back and display our heels. My companion laughed, put his arm round my shoulder and said Allah would protect us. I fervently hoped he would and started praying to Muhammad's God for the first time in my life.

The man with the lamp nucleized terror, like a grain of sand in an oyster. More so because the encounter had been entirely innocuous. It was the uncertainty of what might happen in the next minute; the

*Literal translation — market in which wives are bought and sold.

spectrum of possibilities stretching out before us, made each step I took seem quite heroic and sickeningly fearsome. It might not be a mere stick the next time round, someone might see before we had a chance to ... The questions might not be quite so easy to answer. Perhaps there would be no questions at all. There could be a booby trap five feet away, we might be walking into it right now.

The more these thoughts hurled round in my head, the more I came to regret the recklessness with which I had decided upon the enterprise. If I were to die, how would Pamela find out? When I did not return after a week or a fortnight or even a month, she would just have to assume that ... On the other hand, she might think that I had been taken prisoner, that there was a chance I might be released if she approached the right authorities. After all, technically I could claim protection from the British Consulate. But this is not a party game, getting lost in the fairground. There was a kind of war going on, I should have had the sense to stay out of it all. If a bomb went off right now, there would be two bodies lying dead on the field. Who would ever know? How soon would we be discovered? By all accounts there were hundreds, even thousands of such bodies lying round the place. And we looked no different from any other villager, in fact we had taken great care to disguise ourselves.

Every sound shook me. The fireflies knocked holes in my heart; every time one of those beastly creatures blinked, I conjured up a *razakar* or a Mukti Fauj guerilla, out on his night patrol. The crescent moon hung in a clear sky casting a thin film of light around. Stars winked, crickets chirped, occasionally an owl hooted. We crossed a narrow bamboo bridge over a shallow stream, trudged slowly on, sometimes in ankle-deep slush, more often in thigh-high water. The night seemed endless, stubborn, congealed, refusing to drift away. Insects talked with the dark in a low electronic hum. And I saw that speck again on my mind's screen, rushing at me now, loud, threatening to leap into three-dimensional reality in the approaching minute, the very next second: Death.

Abdul said, 'It will be safer in the morning, when the sun comes up. These trouble-makers, they all prowl around at night.'

'Thanks,' I screamed, 'thanks for telling me now.' Why the hell had we come in the dark in that case?

Abdul explained we could not afford to be seen passing through the same village twice. And during the day a field could be just as dangerous as a village road. If we got to Comilla before dawn, we would be safe. The guerillas would have retired behind the border or else be dug into their hideouts; the *razakars* would have gone to bed after a night's duty. The first couple of hours after dawn were a time of unspoken truce. We would be able to walk through the villages, perhaps even talk to a few people without arousing suspicion.

The moon swam out of the sky, darkness thickened and my feet ached. I thought of all those millions of homeless, hungry, hunted men and women, wading through mud and nettles for days on end, leaving behind all they prized most. People who had had no choice, who had witnessed death and butchery, whose minds were numb with shock. The small things they must have left behind on the roadside, a child's rattle perhaps, a woman's earring. Unsuspected traps they must have encountered, casualties en route, friends and loved ones they had had to abandon to save their own lives. The reckless destruction of homes, burning huts, flaming haystacks, bony cows lying dead in a field for want of food. Infants who could not even speak, torn from their mother's breasts and mercilessly slaughtered. Horrors which eclipsed imagination, the total unreality of it all — that men could do these things to one another.

My mind swung erratically from the personal to the general. I did not know how many hours we had walked but it felt unendurably long. I trudged on like an automaton, one step after another, trusting my companion to lead the way. But those last few miles were quite unreal. Here I was walking into something which others had died to avoid. These fields, that stream, the mango grove we had just passed through — the scene of tragedy, deaths, perhaps running into hundreds. Hunger, disease, an odd bullet or the farmer's scythe that put an end to so many hopes and loves. Would I ever come out of this lion's lair? Or would I merely add another digit to that inconceivable number of stricken lives nipped in their prime? If my mission did succeed, what results would I show? How would it weigh in the balance? Is any action worth a human life?

Dawn came abruptly, a sudden flash of gold and then the sun. There was green all round us, coconut trees, banana plants and bamboo groves. The village was near, another half mile or so. My *lungi* was soaked in slush, my feet pricked and bleeding. But I drew the strong morning air into my lungs and heaved a sigh. If we had managed to come this far, we might even make it the whole way. There was not a being in sight, no animals, just fields and trees and the incessant squawking of crows.

When we got to Chok Bazar, on the outskirts of Comilla, there were a few people moving about but we didn't seem to attract much attention. From what we could see, the town had been shelled, most likely by the Indians. But Abdul forbade me to ask the passers-by — we would be instantly spotted as strangers and handed over. So I held my curiosity at bay and agreed to retrace my steps, this time through the villages. If questioned, we would say we were passing through, had spent the night in Comilla and were now returning to Bibir Bazar (conveniently close to the Indian border) where we lived.

Our first stop on the return journey was Jagannathpur, a one-time predominantly Hindu village. And here I had my first vision of the scale of destruction 'these Punjabi beasts' had perpetrated. There were hardly any huts or stone buildings left standing, not a soul around, except an old man who sat hunched up on the porch of what must have once been his home. Whole streets had been burnt down, scarred bamboo, sheets of rusty iron and rubble lay across our path. The Hindu temple which gave the village its name had been all but demolished: gaping holes embroidered by charred wood, broken walls and the sacred idol lying in a hundred broken pieces on the ground. It was here that Abdul's pace quickened, his face showed signs of apprehension.

When we had passed through and he was his old self again, I asked him why. 'In a deserted village, how would we explain what we were doing? If anyone had seen us ...' Yes, I understood, it was a near miss.

By now I had become accustomed to a few questioning glances, a sprinkling of 'Shalaam Alikum's and even the odd brief chat with one of Abdul's acquaintances or distant relations. One woman said, 'There are no Hindus left in the village. The young women they took away, men and old women they shot or threw into the stream.' Another lady, with a clay pitcher on her head, whispered news about one of Abdul's distant cousins: 'They threw the two-month old infant into the fire when it started screaming as they were dragging Kishwar (the mother) away.'

But it was in the next village that I had my christening in terror. From a distance we could see hosts of vultures, huge ugly birds leaping over one another. As we came closer, I saw the focus of their attention. It was a freshly dug trench, about ten feet wide and as deep, the dumping ground for human bodies. The air stank, bones and skulls lay scattered all about. And the central point of all this activity must have contained some corpses which still had flesh on them. The scavengers covered the whole ground, one on top of another, at least a hundred of them. Their raucous cries cut into the still morning air, the horrendous jubilation of these death-loving monsters deafened my ears.

I turned away, terrified and stunned. I had never witnessed a man dying. Nor had I ever beheld a decomposing body. Then suddenly, these wide-winged birds, tearing at each other, scattering bones from the air, plucking out lumps of human flesh — I felt my stomach heave, the ground spinning under me.

'Takes less space this way,' Abdul said. 'When the birds have done their work, there will be only dry bones. Then the military will come and fill it up with earth.'

PART THREE

5

Retchings of a Soured Cynic

I always thought I was a fairly brutal
realist, but I am beginning to suspect
that the whole thing is a pose to hide the
sentimental preacher.

REINHOLD NIEBUHR

Returning to England induced a feeling of loss. Reality had been taken away, as if one was revisiting a dream. Suspended above the ground by an invisible force whose strength was absolute and character unknown, one tried to climb down and touch the earth. But the most desperate efforts yielded no results. With time, gravity, the sheer pressure of daily living, would pull one down of course, but at a pace over which one had no control.

This curious sensation seizes me every time I come back to this country, especially after a visit to India. This time it was reinforced by mother's death and the horror of Bangladesh. Helplessly, I move about in a fog, seeing people in blurred outlines, hearing their voices at one remove, as if they were echoes in a well. Simple acts take on a spectral aspect, contact becomes tenuous and readjustment to the old familiar locale is an extended exercise in sleep-walking from which I am roused in slow imperceptible stages. Till one day the fog lifts, the voices shed their cloying echoes and I walk on solid ground once more.

It cannot be the fact of my foreignness that provokes these responses. For I have visited and lived in many other countries — France, America, Scandinavia. But nowhere else have I experienced this feeling of suspension, a strange disconnection verging on the schizoid.

Nor is it due to the barrier of language. For though my mother-tongue is Bengali, in the sense that the first words I ever spoke were in that language, I am now far more intimate with the language of this country. I think and write only in English, and any attempt to speak in Bengali is initially always an effort in translation.

The obvious differences in social structure between the land of my birth and the country I have adopted do not offer a clue either. For I have spent all my adult years in the West and my present life-style bears no resemblance to that of my family. In fact I find the other set of mores irksome; it is always an immense relief to get away. There is no incipient chauvinism in my personality either; I feel no more intensely Indian than British. When I changed my passport to go to Portugal — the Indian and Portuguese governments have had no diplomatic connections since the military conquest of Goa — it made no emotional impact on me whatsoever: one sheaf of papers exchanged for another.

Yet this very real estrangement persists. I feel alienated rather than an alien, though there is a fair crop of incidental stimuli which induces the latter feeling as well, at times. I don't know what effects these episodes have on the deeper levels of the psyche but I suspect they are not central to the main problem. Principally, they are connected with race and colour. And that is why I live in Hampstead, which is an area of London where certain decent liberal assumptions are shared by the mass of the community, even though individual acts defying those assumptions do sometimes occur. I am aware that Hampstead is an unusual enclave, rather like a sealed hothouse in the middle of a ferocious winter. I prefer to live in it precisely because I need to be nurtured; I do not have the resilience to withstand the hailstones of prejudice and the deep frost of ostracism which I would encounter in the outer space of mainstream British life.

But it is just as well to get the surface irritations out of the way and answer the rhetorical question: 'But surely, you yourself aren't subjected to any prejudice round here?' Yes I am, and all the more hurtfully because it comes when least expected, because I don't go looking for it and all too often make the blinkered assumption that it doesn't exist. An incident occurs which rudely reminds you that you are a foreigner, that the natives resent you and most people don't subscribe to *New Statesman* values. Your first reaction is one of outrage, as if you were a white British liberal yourself, and one of your own countrymen had assaulted the bastion of decency of which you are guardian. But soon outrage dissolves into self-pity and then suppurating hate. You look with new eyes at your most trusted British friend. Suspicion enters the system; you become unaccountably aggressive towards the most well-meaning social acquaintance.

Days go by, weeks, perhaps even months. You rationalize, talk yourself out of the siege mentality, see the folly of your ways in taking one solitary episode as indicative of common feeling. In the understanding company of friends you lose your newly acquired abrasiveness; you are back to your old self again, jolly, able to take a joke against yourself, even one of those racialist ones. Then suddenly, without warning, another incubating Enoch strikes a punch in your face in the dark. And the whole process repeats itself, but with this difference — each fresh indignity leaves behind a residue of bile and distrust which cannot be dug out even by the most analytic mental machinery.

Years after my arrival in Britain, I was having a drink with a girl in a pub when a man, obviously in his cups, came over and sat at our table, uninvited. He did a weak imitation of the Peter Sellers accent by way of introduction and proceeded to ask a question. 'What are the two English words you people learn when you first come to this country?'

Before I could muster a reply, the man answered his own query, 'National Assistance'.

My muscles tensed, the cigarette trembled in my hands and the gentleman continued, 'Just off the ship and then run to the Exchange, as if they had the trots. Not the likes of you, mind. You are educated.'

I was tempted to tell him that I had been on the dole myself, not because I was all that ravenous about 'money, money' as he put it, but simply because no employer would give me a job. But that was ten years earlier; besides he wouldn't get the point anyway. So I let it go.

How did he support himself? *Worked* for a living, he did, as a porter in the store next door. And all those large shots of whisky? Oh, he always put a few bob on the horses. 'We tolerate you, make no mistake. Without the National Assistance, you'd all be dying like rats.' I wondered if he was having me on. But no, the tone of moral certitude and superiority was unmistakable.

Someone had told him all this, I thought to myself. He hadn't figured it out all by himself. Some editorial, some clever little newspaper report, some television 'documentary' — the insidious telepathy of Enoch Powell at work in all those myriad cubicles.

Once more the clouds gathered round me, the constant need to have to defend oneself against implicit accusations. One was being watched, there was an insistent awareness that all one's actions had to be models of behaviour lest a whole community be blamed for them. One was no longer an individual. Hence the indignity of having to keep a smile on one's lips while a foul-mouthed drunk indulged his inadequacies with grotesque malice. 'Mustn't have a chip on your shoulder, old boy,' I heard my Hampstead friends whisper in my ear. 'If you go out looking for anything, it will always be there.'

Alas, one doesn't have to look; the acid is in the air, invisible and pervasive. For a coloured man the flow of adrenalin is constant, the atmosphere always charged, waiting for a spark to trigger off the explosion: unspoken censure at the tobacconist, the curt turn-around of a pretty girl at a party. Of course the porter wasn't 'representative', the 'reports' tell me he isn't. But personal experiences *aren't* always representative, and the unrepresentative ones hit home just as hard.

One late September evening I was walking up Primrose Hill in Hampstead. There was a first chill of autumn in the air, an uncertain dusk silhouetted the trees on top of the hill, there were no pedestrians on the road. Occasionally a car whizzed past, up to the top of the hump, then vanishing into the trough below. On my left a whole row of houses was half-demolished, about to make way for an estate of de luxe flats for rising young executives. On my right was the hill, deserted except for a solitary man with a dog, way out on the other side. In the far distance, the Post Office Tower dutifully kept guard over London, blinking. There was a strange quiet all round, a nice sort of feeling for the first drink of the day. I was walking to the Queen's at the foot of the hill on Regent's Park Road.

Suddenly, a small stone hit me in the back. I looked round, startled, and a burst of children's laughter greeted me. I couldn't make out how many they were, but I could see a group, small in height, some fifty yards away. 'What the devil ...' I shouted, and took a step or two in their direction. Instantly, the single stone was followed by a second, then a third, till I was faced with a veritable shower. Not all of them reached me, but a few did. As my legs began to falter, their resolution hardened. Chanting a doggerel,

> *Dirty wog, dirty wog,*
> *Shove 'im down your mother's bog*

the whole group started towards me.

I was furious, a little daunted by the stones but unshaken in my determination to teach these brats a lesson. I didn't quite know what I would do, perhaps give them a severe talking to or some such thing. The thought of anything physical never entered my head; slap their faces or bang their heads together — the notion of some kind of teacher-like punishment did not cross my mind. They were a bunch of kids after all, indulging in a nasty prank. That was all, surely. I was not the least bit afraid, not then.

Then the shower of stones became heavier, more of them hit the target than missed it, the gap between me and the group began to close. My pace slackened while theirs quickened. There was no one else around, no houses on either side of the road. The lamp-post was a good fifty yards away. The dark had thickened, blotting out the solitary man on the hill with his dog.

I shouted some ineffectual command such as, 'Stop this nonsense before I ...' with the assumed voice of adult authority. But the only response was laughter and a louder, more cynical rendering of their warlike chant. When they came up to me, I was a good deal less sure of myself than I had been a couple of minutes earlier. 'Now, what's this all about?' I asked firmly, trying to sound composed and unintimidated. Once again all I got was a peal of raucous laughter.

There were some six in the group, the youngest one could not have been more than eight, the oldest about twelve or thirteen. The only girl in the company still clutched a few stones in her hand. The oldest boy, the leader of the band, came forward and flashed a self-satisfied grin at me: 'Heh mister, why don't ya pull ya traasers down and run?'

'Now look ...' I shouted, and took a step towards him.

And then he took out this thing from his pocket and flicked it open. 'Yah,' he said, still grinning, pointing it at me. In the weak light I could see it was only a medium-sized penknife. But that was poor consolation. I took a step back, the boy took one forward; I did the same again, and he too repeated his performance. I was scared, and I knew he had sensed it.

Just then a car came rushing up the hill from the other side, with headlamps in full glow. For a moment the penknife and the boy halted in apparent confusion. I shrieked, 'Help!' at the top of my lungs, whirled round and started running. In the few moments the boy and the group waited to see if the car would stop, I had gained a start of some ten yards. When the car was gone and the race resumed, I was literally running for my life, while they were indulging in a sadistic chase. Naturally, I ran faster. A few stones hit me, but they were feathers compared to the vision of that penknife in my back.

The whole encounter could not have lasted more than about five to seven minutes. But it seemed a good deal longer to me at the time. I have never felt more like a hunted animal than I did that evening. When I entered the pub, sweat-faced and shaking, a solicitous young acquaintance, carrying the banner of white British liberalism in his fist, said, 'You look beat. Let me get you a drink.'

I threw him a hateful look and replied, 'No thanks. I prefer to buy my own.'

Neither too little nor too much should be made of such episodes. There is a way of underplaying them which is both hypocritical and naive. On the one hand there is the middle-class coloured immigrant himself who tends to dismiss them with a laugh, treating them as isolated pimples on the smooth hospitable skin of British life. This they are decidedly not. Rather, they are manifestations of a widely shared ethos among indigenous inhabitants of these islands whose origins can be traced back to Curzon, Macaulay and beyond.

The dilemma which faces the middle-class coloured immigrant is indeed a complex one and deserves investigation. The immigrant intellectual has made his way up to the middle-class haven by a process precisely calculated to set him apart from his fellow countrymen. He has abandoned the ethos and culture of the country which spawned him in the honest convicton that the alternative offered by his hosts is superior: that individual life is worth more than lip service to a dead creed; that human misery needs to be dealt with here and now, rather than indulgently relegated to a hereafter; that reason and analysis are preferable to dogma and priestly dictations. His intellectual structure is based on liberal assumptions which appear self-evidently more attractive than, say, the hierarchical notion of Man's lot enshrined in caste.

So, just as the convert is a more zealous proselytizer than those who were born into the faith, the immigrant intellectual seeks to trumpet his newly-acquired ideology. In social terms, this leads him to shun the company of his fellow countrymen for fear his white liberal friends will class him with the others and all his heroic intellectual efforts will have been in vain. Not that he is a parvenu. Indeed, he feels genuine contempt for the ideas and habits of the others who came from his motherland. But it is a short ride from this fortress of condescension to an attitude of bigotry and prejudice — the very stance his liberal professions condemn. If he were white, the hatred would not be so strong. But because he is black or brown, and looks and sounds just like the others, the immigrant intellectual is often the most colour-prejudiced man around. (In much the same way as a working-class intellectual who finally makes it to the Savile Club tends to be the most vehement spokesman of the Right.)

Immediately on my arrival in Britain, I was told by a young Indian poet, who had then gained some notoriety on the London literary scene, that he had never once experienced any prejudice or colour-discrimination in all the years he had lived here. 'All these stories you read in the papers,' he confided, 'all cooked up by journalists, chasing after copy. No one gives a damn if you're black or brown, so long as you've got something to offer.' This, barely two years after the Notting Hill Gate riots.

Of course, the poet was trying to reassure me; in effect he was saying, 'You'll be all right old chap, so long as you don't try to rock the boat. If you're a bright young lad, and successfully manage to ape your white peers in thought, speech and behaviour, you've nothing to worry about. Look at me, I'm not discriminated against.'

Thus does the Establishment quench dissent and muffle rebellion. If you are a member of an under-privileged minority and the pillars of society single you out to receive the fruits of privilege, you are hardly likely to be the vociferous claimant for justice towards the rest of your brethren. The very qualifications which make you an acceptable representative of your people in white society at large are the ones which will prevent you from being an honest spokesman, demanding those fundamental rights and freedoms and opportunities which should be the birthright of every human being on earth. For a coloured man to admit that he is the target of prejudice is to confess failure, the ultimate inability to integrate totally with white society. For in the end, no matter how you wear your hair or your tie, wherever you may have your clothes tailored, and however polished your accent, you will always be black or brown according to the genes you inherited. However much you are like your white friends in all other respects, the obvious external distinction will always remain. And as long as the social ethos around you dictates that 'darker the skin, more inferior the man', you will never avoid being the victim of ostracism, prejudice and worse. If a coloured man tells me he has never experienced discrimination in this country, he has either confined himself to a very restricted enclave, and not moved about even in London, let alone the rest of the country. Or alternatively he is telling a lie — either to me or, what is much worse, to himself.

There is another way of minimizing the importance of such instances, and this is adopted on the other side of the fence, by the white liberal intelligentsia itself. And it is far more irksome to stomach because it neatly avoids the central issue — the root cause of discrimination — by appearing to be fervently left-wing, infected with a messianic zeal to improve the lot of the underdog.

The thesis runs roughly as follows: 'My dear fellow, we all know these things happen, and it is unfortunate that they do. In an ideal society, *no one* should have to put up with such humiliation. We all accept that. But as it happens, we don't live in an ideal society. And if we're going to change the one we've got into something more compassionate and humane, then we've got to get our priorities right. And we've got to decide whether it's more important to be worked up about a pub incident with a drunk than trying to ensure that thousands of West Indian teenagers who've just left school get the jobs they deserve. Surely, if we're going to get exercised about discrimination, then the problem of the British born school-leaver with five O-levels, who is told to go and sweep the streets, is far more socially disturbing than your encounter with a bunch of nasty kids on Primrose Hill Road. Mind you, I am not condoning the behaviour of those kids, nor am I suggesting that you should take it lying down. But you must see that against the larger social canvas, the bright school-leaver who can't get a job because he is black must be of much greater concern than the pranks of half a dozen school children. After all, there is the possibility, isn't there, that if you were a tramp, and white as they come, they'd still have set upon you. And perhaps the incident demonstrates, not so much prejudice, as the innate sadism of children. *You were there*, so you were a target, and you were brown. But it could have been somebody else, don't you think?'

At a glance the argument is persuasive. And it generally has the effect of shutting up the complaining immigrant. In one blow it attacks two of the most vulnerable areas of his personality. Firstly, it activates an incipient guilt which is never far from his consciousness. He is better off than thousands of others who share his disability, and he does or is seen to do nothing about improving *their* lot. Instead, he goes around grumbling about a trivial little incident, which causes him no greater discomfort than a sudden profusion of sweat. Compared with the miseries of starvation and joblessness, how great are the burdens our middle-class immigrant bears? Is he not the recipient of privilege while his fellow coloureds ...?

Secondly, it panders to his vanity by implying an equality of social and intellectual status between the white liberal and the coloured immigrant. The plaintiff is told, 'Look, except for the fact that this unfortunate incident happened to you, wouldn't you be saying exactly the same things yourself? You think and feel the same way as I do, what's the difference between us? If you can detach yourself for a moment from this specific situation, you will see the sense of my arguments.'

It is a seductive ploy and nearly always fells the victim.

The flaws in the argument are not only those of logic, but more importantly of illiberal and offensive assumptions masquerading as radical concern. The hypothetical comparison between the middle-class coloured immigrant and the white tramp is insulting because there is an implicit assertion that each of them constitutes an undesirable element in the community. The parallel would not be drawn between a white burgher and the white tramp for the simple reason that with all 'the innate sadism of children' in the world, such an incident would never happen to the former. In seeking to neutralize the colour confrontation by introducing the imaginary white tramp, our liberal is condoning a social ethos in which discrimination is endemic, whether it is directed against the black or the vagrant, both of whom are socially vulnerable.

The other ploy of 'getting our priorities right' is equally mischievous in that it deflects attention from the particular and shifts the onus of guilt onto the immigrant himself, with a call for *greater* social concern for the underdog. It dictates that one should be more irked by a general social malaise than a specific injustice within one's own experience. It obscures the fact that both phenomena — the jobless British-born West Indian and the middle-class immigrant who is stoned on Primrose Hill Road — spring from the same cause: British society in the main believes that coloured men are inferior.

It is true that black slums, joblessness and destitution pose social problems of far greater magnitude than an instance of white kids throwing stones at *a* black man. But the individual's reaction to the latter need be no less intense for that. My sense of social injustice is necessarily conditioned by what I have come to expect of that society. And my grievance is not placated by the assurance that there are people worse off than I am. It is ridiculous and dangerously Utopian to ask me to feel less hurt by a pinching nail in my shoe because millions of people walk about barefoot in India. The white liberal conscience may be appeased by such manipulative logic, my anger is not.

Above all, the biggest myth that requires demolition seeks to convey such instances of prejudice as sporadic and unrepresentative. But the experience of the coloured immigrant is exactly converse. Minor incidents of discrimination are not unique occurrences but the staple fare of his life. And because he is thus incessantly bombarded he develops a protective skin which enables him at first to ignore, then cease to feel the darts that are constantly thrown at him. The objective, albeit unconscious, of the white liberal polemic is achieved, the middle-class coloured immigrant is silenced, and once again the exploiter and the exploited acquiesce in a conspiracy to maintain the status quo.

In his ferocious monograph *Portrait of the Anti-Semite* (1948) Jean-Paul Sartre identified the principal element in anti-semitic thinking as being a psychological deficiency rather than the professed product of economic and social frictions. He said that the bourgeois, unable to define himself in his environment, has a ready-made 'other' in the form of a Jew, on whom he can unload all his personal inadequacies.

Sartre argued that in periods of economic depression, the powers-that-be have always needed a scapegoat, not only to explain away the visible hunger and destitution in the outside world. They have also needed an internal scapegoat, something every individual may observe and identify as his own personal salvation. Because, once the cushions normally offered in an exploitative society are withdrawn, the bourgeois, lacking any internal resources, is left defenceless, staring at a cipher which may well be himself.

In times such as these, the Jew — at least in Europe — has proverbially provided the most handy solution to the collapsing psyche both in individual and national terms. 'Look, there goes the Jew! I am superior to him, therefore I exist!' And again: 'Do you know why our factories are empty, prices are rising in the shops, and there is no food at the greengrocer's? Because the Jew has bagged all the money and bought up everything. That is why we have to exterminate him because he is against the national and social good. Once we get rid of him, all our problems will be over.'

The explanation need have no connection with reality. Indeed, since it originates in a psycho-pathological state of mind, it is almost necessary that it should have a large measure of fantasy, of paranoia and personal insecurity, masquerading as rational exegesis. Thus it is impossible to refute either in debate or empirical demonstration. 'No anti-Semite,' says Sartre, 'has ever been converted.'

Although this is a too-rigid Marxist-existentialist analysis of anti-semitism, we may usefully find some strands in the thesis which would apply to the phenomenon of colour-prejudice in Britain.

The sleight of hand performed by the ruling class over the workers in this country during the last one hundred and fifty years provides the closest historical analogy. At the inception of the British colonial empire, which luckily for this country, happened roughly to coincide with the Industrial Revolution, a number of shrewd businessmen and politicians went abroad to establish a hegemony, which lasted till the middle of this century, over coloured peoples the world over.

Exploitation was simultaneously carried out on two fronts, though those who were exploited on either of these fronts would hardly band together and call each other brothers. The first was the emergent proletariat, the necessary and urgent fodder for the newly discovered and ravenous industrial machine. The condition of workers in industrial Britain during the whole of the nineteenth century was abominable, both in absolute and relative terms.

But there was another group of men, indeed sometimes whole nations, who were equally ruthlessly exploited. The difference between the two groups, apart from the obvious physiognomic ones, was that one group — the white workers slaving away at factories and cotton mills — was told that they were superior *en bloc* to the other.

Thus did the Establishment psychologically placate and justify the degrading conditions of the worker 'in England's green and pleasant land' by loudly and incessantly proclaiming that there were people worse off than he (the kafirs and niggers in those hot and humid far off lands), while keeping its hands tightly closed round the fruits of labour produced by both these groups of unfortunate men.

In Sartrian terms, the factory labourer in Sheffield, lacking identity in his own work, was able to define himself as the superior, civilized white man in contrast to the brown-skinned native in India or the ape-like pigmy in the African jungle. All this was of course overlaid by the so-called civilizing veneer of religion and culture. But basically the message was simple: since *some* white men had gone out and subjugated hundreds and thousands of black and brown natives, therefore by extension it followed that *every* white man was superior to *every* black or brown man.

This enabled the white worker to accept his own inhuman lot a little more complacently. And since it was helpful to the ruling and exploiting elite, the concept of white racial superiority was allowed to seep deep into the ethos of this nation and has remained part of the Western mental outlook ever since, either overtly or subconsciously.

There has been a long line of eulogists for legitimizing this depravity in intellectual mores, all the way from Macaulay and Curzon down to Kipling, Churchill and a quasi-Roman orator in our own times. Significantly, it has never been argued that these men were and are anything but civilized; it was their *opinions* that at times were perhaps a little awry.

The tragedy is that people who have suffered from such *opinions*, or experienced similar fates in different hands, and who might be expected to attempt to remove the social and spiritual inequities that such attitudes breed, are precisely those who, by inclination and by their own experience, are shown up to be the most staunch supporters of the exploitative regime.

There is nothing more fierce than the Irish navvy's hatred of the West Indian; no one who radiates 'I'm-all-right-Jack' more effusively than the South African Jew towards the coloured population; no insect more odoriferous than the Indian shopkeeper in Kenya who talks of 'these bloody niggers' not knowing their place.

Whenever I have launched, at a party in Hampstead, into a diatribe about colour-prejudice, the person who has patiently and exasperatedly tried to tell me that 'these things don't happen' and that I was unnecessarily carrying a chip on my shoulder, has invariably been one or other of my Jewish intellectual friends.

Except once, when it was an affluent Indian businessman.

6

The Collector

> ... to be an artist, and especially an
> expatriate artist, is to be a lonely
> conspirator and ... conspiracy, once it
> becomes a habit, is portable.
>
> V. S. PRITCHETT

Not long after I had returned from Bangladesh, the telephone rang at my house in Hampstead, London. A male voice on the other end of the line introduced itself in fluent, if ornate, Bengali. 'I have the pleasure, Sir, of being ... your humble servant. I have diligently perused your books. Please very much excuse my intrusion if I desire your permission to make a visitation in person.'

Taken unawares as I was, with my knowledge of the vernacular being less than equal to that of my prospective protégé, I did not burst out laughing. Instead, I replied, 'Where do you come from?'

'I am a mixed-up being. My heart is in one place, my soul in another. I am a refugee from Bangladesh.'

I was aware of the nuances; I knew how swift and soft and tortuous the Bengali language could be. For a moment I was stupefied. A torn and lacerated soul? A man without a country? (Epithets which had been fulsomely, if incorrectly, applied to me.) My instant impulse had been to put the phone down. I have enough problems of my own. Another crank. If he wants anything why doesn't he go out and get it himself? Why me?

Yet there was another part of myself which wouldn't let go. I suppose I could explain it as 'novelistic curiosity', a search for material. But honestly, that wouldn't be enough. For I have in me a hunger to know as well as consume. I am not uninterested, I cannot be just a camera. I believe the artist who says he is merely watching is a liar.

I said, 'Well, perhaps we should get together sometime.'

'Yes,' replied my learned disciple, unaccountably switching to English, 'why not in the manner of that Sino-Italianate bard, Ezra?'

'And what manner is that?' I asked squeamishly, hovering between apprehensive ignorance and defiant condescension.

'Imbibation of the nectar of fluids, scotch whisky, ha, ha ... I have discoursed lengthily at my students about the manner of your alcoholic habitats.'

'Habitats' put me out a little, as my wife had recently shovelled out an extraordinary sum of money for a piece of furniture I could have *made* for a quarter of the price. But the gist of the message got through all right. And I have never been one to turn down a drink.

So I said, 'I think that's a very good idea.'

'Marvellously magnificent,' the Bangladesh refugee replied. 'When I shall have the honour of presenting myself at your gracious abode?' Then, without a moment's pause, reverting to colloquial Bengali, 'I do not have the address, only your telephone number. Where do you live?'

I was less than sharp on this one, having fancied myself for being quick on the uptake. I blurted out the number of the house and name of the street. Then the date was fixed and the time. When I put the phone down I had the honour of saying to myself, 'I shall now have the momentous privilege of receiving a Bangladesh refugee in my dilapidated dwelling place.'

Of course, I talked it over with Pamela. 'Why do I go on doing this kind of thing? I know I should have said, "Thanks for ringing, but I can't see you right now, I am busy on a book." I reckon he is stupid into the bargain. Why do I go on indulging in this sort of idiotic nonsense?'

She said, 'You may be less selfish than you make yourself out to be. Perhaps all of you is not a writer. Anyway, you go to the pub often enough, an hour or two with a few drinks won't make all that much difference will it? Besides, you don't even know if he is stupid or not. You'd just like to think he is. You're prejudiced.'

On the appointed day my guest arrived at the house and offered profuse greetings in his native tongue. The man was balding, in his early forties, and exuded an aura of sleazy confidence — if he had been a victim of Yahya Khan's atrocities, it was not apparent from either his manner or his appearance. As usual I was nervous. My fellow countryman on the other hand, having squared himself in the armchair, unleashed an avalanche of words in polished Bengali which left me bemused.

I blathered, 'Sorry, we are out of whisky, but may I offer you a sherry instead?' as if I was the accused, in need of defence.

'Yes, anything,' the refugee replied graciously. 'I do not mind at all, accustomed as I am in the manner of accommodating many aspects of the Western civilization.'

I took it for what it was worth at the time, an urbane conciliatory gesture. After all, whisky had been specifically mentioned in our last conversation; I could have popped out and got a bottle. In a sense I had slipped up as a host. But hours later I paused to reflect that it was I who had been doing him a favour, yet within minutes of his arrival he had managed to make me feel squeamish, as if I bore the burden of blame in some indefinable but pervasive manner.

'You are master of writing arts,' said my acquaintance. 'You are in sure possession of the most profound knowledge about English language.'

The fact is I like flattery, since I get it so infrequently, and I replied, 'Well, it's very nice of you to say so ... but ... er ...'

'Exactly rightly,' he continued. 'I am compulsioned to believe in you because there is no one else like your good self. In one breath you have created being out of clay. Before you there was nothing, after you life.'

Despite the greasy vulgarity, this kind of praise is not easy to slough off, especially if one is convinced that one is under-recognized. But that is no excuse for being led off the scent. The percipience of the artist consists in being precisely right. Being near right or just a little wrong must never be a consolation. So, fly in the spider's web, I queried, 'And what can I do for you?'

'All in a moment,' quoth he, 'I see your greatness. You are witness to the light. You know.'

I was beginning to feel a little queasy by this stage, so I asked, 'What light?'

'Ha ... ha ...' he replied, 'you deny yourself. Humorousness, I see. But it is not necessary. I am writer, I understand. Bandopadhya, Chatterjee, Tagore ... I am in that tradition. I must be made known. It is shallow this Western world. I do not know the ways to travel on its roads. You are here, that is why I have selected you. You will translate all my writings and the world will know me through you. You are indeed fortunate.'

Stunned, I drew away and spent the rest of the evening boozing in a pub. Friends asked me what the matter was. I remember replying, with grey abandon, 'Nothing really. Just that I've been presented with a chip to wear on my shoulder.'

But the alcohol did not wash away a nagging uneasiness. The man was either a primeval simpleton or Felix Krull in person. Certainly, he was no ordinary *babu* freshly hatched from one of the BA (plucked) batteries which pass for universities in the sub-continent. During our little chat he had given me a résumé of his career which would have been impressive under different circumstances.

His wife was a doctor, had been called to attend on West Pak Army officers during the troubles and was still living at home in Dacca. He himself was a writer of repute in the vernacular, with eleven published books to his name and an audience running into hundreds of thousands. He was evasive about how he had managed to smuggle himself out of East Pakistan (as it then was), nor did he clarify, at the beginning of our conversation, the purpose of his visit to England. How was he supporting himself here? Who had paid his fare out? How had he managed to get hold of me? These questions spun around as an intuitive conviction began to harden in my mind — there was more to it than mere verbal bombast from a Western Oriental Gentleman. I was sure I was going to see the man again.

I was not wrong. After a statutory period of two months — presumably to let me recover from the initial shock of first exposure — the telephone brought his voice to my ears again. This time I was on guard and fielded his queries with masterly calculation.

How was I? Fine, thank you. How was the writing going? Ditto. Over the next five minutes I gave him my opinion about the state of the universe, my psychic circumstances and the literary predicament in general: they were all fine. I felt it would involve an unnecessary expenditure of time if I were to return his felicitous enquiries, item for item, as I figured that he would volunteer any information which went against the all-round fineness I had projected about my own condition.

As it turned out, it was not quite like that. If I had a straight flush, he turned up a royal one. Since that last meeting our Bangladesh refugee had moved into Hampstead, got himself a job on a national daily at over three thousand pounds a year and was whizzing around in a four-wheeler. Would I and my wife care to come over for dinner at his humble abode? 'Curiouser and curiouser,' I reflected. And being of an empirical turn of mind, I resolved to investigate the facts. So I accepted the invitation.

It was then that the trap was sprung. Since the grand date was still a few days away, would I care to meet his 'girl friend' (the word was pronounced with the appropriate degree of spinsterish demureness) before that? Perhaps they could both come round to our place this Friday, if that was all right?

'But of course,' I replied, strung between an insane curiosity and self-deprecating fury. 'I should have thought of this,' I said to myself. 'Poor dumb fool that I am. The fellow is a pathological liar, obviously, a con man of the first water. Imagine a refugee from Bangladesh getting a job on a national daily! Can't even speak English straight, let alone ... And three thousand pounds at that. Ah well, isn't worth getting worked up over a thing like this. A load of fantasy, that's what it is. A car into the bargain, I ask you. Really! And in Hampstead too! I mean I am not a snob or anything like that, but it does take a bit of spare cash to move into this area of town, you know.' What I couldn't figure out was why the man had bothered to put this line over to me. After all, what could he hope to gain by ...

I was to find out soon enough.

Friday arrived. I told Pamela I was expecting a Bangladesh refugee and his girl friend that evening. She asked, 'Shall we light the fire in the sitting room or do you want to have them round in the kitchen?'

'Well, I don't know,' I replied, not having pondered such mundane details. 'It's such a bother, isn't it? Getting the coal, clearing out the fireplace and everything ...'

'So we shall have them round in the kitchen, shall we?'

'I didn't say that. What I mean is ...'

The fact is I wasn't sure. When my refugee friend knocked on the door the first time round, I had taken him straight up to the study, and that was that. He had made a professional call; I was not a friend of his, so there was no question of the sitting room or the kitchen. For the difference between the two is symbolic in our house. Either close friends or those we care two damn hoots about usually come into the kitchen. People we wish to impress, middle-class friends and creatures of that ilk we 'entertain' in the sitting room. So there was a bit of a dilemma about our Bengali phoenix and his girl friend. They were making a social visit, and Indian hospitality dictated that the couple be treated accordingly. On the other hand, I was sorely reluctant to extend myself in order to ...

Pamela sensed my pusillanimity and resolved the problem. 'I think I'll light it anyway. It's nice to sit by the fire once in a while, even when there aren't any guests around.'

'Well, in that case ...' I conceded with relief, 'we might as well have them in front of the flames. Doesn't make much odds, does it?'

'No, it doesn't,' she replied, releasing a minute smile from the corner of her lips.

Of course I was irritated with myself, but intrigued as well. *If* all the man had said was true, in the purely material sense he had done a damn sight better in six months than I had in twelve years. And I wasn't going to descend to the lurid level of comparing my talents with his, no thank you! If that couldn't be taken for granted, what could? Yet, a persistent sense of apprehension lingered; I could not settle the issue in my mind. How the hell had he managed to acquire a girl in this time when I had taken ...? Him being married too! At least, when I came to London I was single and young and ... Anyway, talking of his looks, well ... The fact is, where I wished to feel condescension, I experienced throbs of jealousy; where I longed to be in the role of a clinical and amused observer, I had been drawn into passionate combat.

The couple made their appearance punctually at six o'clock. I ushered them into the sitting room, somewhat unnerved by the antipodean accent in the female and the cheshire cat grin on the male. Introductions were completed without second names being mentioned. I offered them sherry — which is what we drink in the house at that time of day — and Pamela joined us a few minutes later.

'Diana is very versed in writing arts, just like your good self,' my compatriot ventured, by way of breaking the ice. 'A most supreme lady.'

'Really, darling,' Diana replied, fluttering her false eyelashes and flashing a full-lipped smile at me. 'Must you?'

Needlessly modest, I thought, as I could sympathize with his effusions and divine the reason for that wide stretched grin. For the supreme lady did possess a few credentials, at least on first inspection. She wore a low-necked, tight-fitting blouse (rather fashionably unfashionable) draped over a pair of firm unsupported breasts. Her skin was smooth, with a hint of bronze on her cheeks. She smiled munificently, with generous outward-turned lips. From her ear lobes hung large Indian rings which balanced a triumphantly seductive anglo-saxon face. But for that nasal twang, a perfectly dishy bird — even if she was on the wrong side of thirty-five.

'What's she doing with *him*?' was the first thought that flashed through my mind. 'Surely, she can get any man she wants ...' Male chauvinist that I am, I was to learn that there are more complex reasons which motivate a female than whose which induce instant erections and floods of saliva in a man.

'I haven't read any of your books but I understand they are great,' Diana said to me.

I smiled. 'Depends a lot on your taste, really,' I replied. 'I don't know who reads my books. Most of my friends don't, that I know. But obviously some people must or else they wouldn't go on selling as they do.'

The Bangladesh refugee made a few disclaiming noises at this point, using hyperbole with reckless abandon. The air congealed with viscous flattery, so I intervened, 'Anyway, I take it that you are a toiler in the same vineyard, Diana?'

'Well, yes, I am a writer. I've been writing for years.'

'And what sort of field are you in?'

'Actually, I write about everything, anything at all that comes my way,' Diana answered with a giggle. 'I'm not choosy.'

'That must be a great help,' Pamela cut in.

'Well actually, it is. I don't mind what I write about so long as I get the bread. I am not at all fussy. In Australia I used to write about Fashion and Women's Lib and the Freaked-out generation — that sort of thing, you know. But here of course they pay so little ... It's mostly the American market right now, that's where it's at, you know.'

The beatific smile on the face of the phoenix had set into a cast by now. He neither spake nor snorted but sat in a trance, devouring the golden words pouring out of the mouth of the supremely unfussy lady.

'And what kind of magazines do you write for?'

'I never really bother about those things,' Diana replied, taking a sip of her sherry. 'Leave it all to my agent. No point in getting uptight when a creep of an editor turns down a fantastic story. So I am not into that scene at all. I just get my cheque every month and I am happy. And I don't care for those critics and reviews either.'

My ears perked up on the word 'review' but Pamela was sharper, 'So you write books as well?'

'Oh yes, quite a few. I write them all the time. Last month I was in India, doing a project on Mrs. Gandhi.'

'What kind of a project was that?' I asked timidly, awed in spite of myself.

'It's going to be called "A Day in the Life of Indira Gandhi".'

'So you met the Prime Minister?'

'Well, not actually, but I nearly did. It was all set up, you see. But then she suddenly flew off to Calcutta while I was in Delhi. And then when I went to Calcutta, on my way to Bangladesh, she was back in Delhi. So I never did get to meet her. But the project is going through anyway. You don't have to speak with a person to know how they spend their day, really.'

I confess I was taken aback a little. The woman was articulate, not at all stupid, but there was a problem of wavelengths — she was transmitting at a frequency I could not receive. I wondered if this displacement was due to her being born in the land of the kangaroos. But my speculations were cut short by the final twist of the knife, her pièce de résistance: 'You know Germaine* of course, you must do. She is a great friend of mine. Mustn't believe a word they say about her round here, she is a wonderful chick, really. You must meet her sometime.'

In all that torrent of words, I could barely squeeze in a reply, 'I would love to ...'

'Yes sure, we'll fix it up soon.' I wasn't given a chance to thank her for the gracious kindness. For with these last words, she promptly rose from her seat, focussed two limpid eyes on her valet and ordained, 'And now darling, we must go.'

Almost a stage exit, I thought, but unexpectedly, pleasantries followed. 'See you on Saturday, hope you don't mind a curry. So nice of you to have had us round this evening. It's been marvellous. Sorry we can't stay longer. Bye!' Swifter than a hurricane, her trailing skirt whirled out of the house, our refugee from Bangladesh dutifully following.

Pamela heaved a sigh as we shut the door. My feelings however were ambiguous, I was curious.

On Saturday evening we were received at the door by Diana herself. She was wearing a long flowing robe made of Indian silk, the same

*Germaine Greer, of *The Female Eunuch* fame.

large earrings and, for my taste, an excessive amount of rouge. 'How nice of you to be so prompt,' she said, by way of a greeting. 'Did you manage to find your way all right? Isn't it infernally cold? How daring of you to wear white in the middle of winter, Sasthi. Let me take your coat, Pamela. The others will be here soon. Come and sit by the fire and warm your hands. Salim is down in the kitchen, putting the finishing touches to the *biriyani*, but he'll be up in a minute. I hate cooking, don't you?'

As no answer was expected, we didn't give any. Instead, I took time off to wonder as to how late was 'punctually late'. For I had expected some comment about my white linen suit but hardly a ticking off for being on time. I was to discover later that I was on the wrong tack as usual. Our hostess had an aversion to *thought*, she said whatever came into her head at the moment, strenuously refusing to let any idea incubate and mature in her brain. The high-speed chatter was a race against time, there was the risk that if left too long without being ejected out of her mouth, some notion or other might take root and the mind would not be as clean and empty as it had been the previous minute.

We were ushered into the sitting room where a languid young man stood in the corner, glass of red wine in his hand. 'This is Jan, Jan Balogh,' Diana said, adding our names to the list with the same formality. 'Jan is a poet, he writes fantastic poetry, don't you darling? He came out of Hungary just after the revolution there, he loves England but thinks he might try the States for a while. And I think that's a marvellous idea. It's a great scene there, only you've got to take it in small doses. And Jan is very avant garde, he doesn't believe in rhymes and things like that. You really must read his poems, they're fantastic, simply fantastic, Sasthi. And I've told him all about you.'

I extended my hand to the poet; he did the same; we shook. His palms were moist, it was a limp handshake. And the same air of unsubstantiality hung about Jan's face, loose blond hair falling over his forehead, wistful blue eyes and thin pink lips. He certainly looked the part — the poet manqué. 'They have something in common, these two,' I thought to myself, and by the glance he gave her when she brushed past him towards the drinks table, I knew what it was. The Hungarian poet and the Australian lady writer had been, perhaps still were, lovers. Diana poured the drinks out of cut glass decanters — sherry, whisky or wine. There were silver ash-trays scattered around, an Afghan carpet on the parquet floor and numerous Indian paintings framed in heavy mahogany. 'An altogether opulent room,' I thought, 'not at all bad for a refugee to land in.' A nasty competitiveness entered my system; bourgeois to bourgeois, I started comparing our house with hers. Predictably, it was an unequal contest — hers won. And I was piqued.

'You live in style, Diana,' I remarked. 'For a change, it's nice to see a fellow writer who owns the house at the top of the hill.'

'You have a lovely house too,' Diana replied, with polite unconviction. 'I loved your fireplace.'

'I'm glad you liked it, but you see, I didn't pay for it and I don't own it. And I don't know many writers who could afford a pad like this either. Must be a nice feeling though, to be financially successful as a writer.'

'Yes it is,' my hostess conceded, without modesty. 'And everyone can, if they put their mind to it. There's no great secret. All you've got to do is do your thing and sock it to them.'

At this point Salim appeared on the scene, apron draped round his waist, sub-butlerian expression on his face. 'How have you been keeping?' he asked in Bengali. I answered politely in English, hoping my point would be taken. But no, skin was thicker than language; the cook sat down next to me on the sofa and began a long monologue in whispered Bengali. Pamela sat in the other corner of the room, silent and amused. Jan, the Hungarian poet, and Diana stood next to the drinks, ostensibly communing about the cosmic significance of unrhymed verse.

The substance of what Salim had to pour into my ears irked as well as astonished me. I dislike confidences at the best of times, but most specifically from strangers. I feel I am being used as a public utility, down which the visiting gent is flushing his unwanted excreta. But Salim's story had such a rivetting air of fantasy that it could almost be true.

He started by stating the obvious. For a refugee, he was doing extraordinarily well, didn't I think? Diana was a kind and hospitable woman, and very attractive too. One couldn't really hope for more, could one? That is why he couldn't understand why his wife was being so intransigent. Salim's face carried an expression of genuine puzzlement and wonder. Naturally, my curiosity rose.

'You see,' he said, 'I am a Muslim, and according to our religion there is nothing wrong with it, nothing at all.'

I was tempted to ask, 'What?' but I resisted the urge. For what he had to say was so far out of my own experience that the imaginative leap required to land in that bizarre territory was not within my physical powers.

'I have already married her, you see,' Salim continued in Bengali. 'We had a few friends round and we declared we were husband and wife. According to Muslim law that is enough. Diana does not mind having my first wife living here as well. She is very co-operative, there are enough rooms in the house, it is an ideal set-up. But being a Bengali girl, my wife in Dacca has strange ideas of her own. She is very backward, a most stubborn woman. She has never been to the West, you see. She just does not understand.'

I felt a chill down my spine, as if I had been suddenly engulfed in a cloud of chloroform. But the Bangladesh refugee went on undeterred.

'She could come here and work in a hospital. Diana would find her a job, she has many contacts, you see. But the pigheaded woman persists in staying on in Dacca, against my express wish. And I just can't get myself to divorce her. It would be easy enough. According to Muslim law, all you have to do is say '*Talak*' three times in succession, and it is done. But women need the security of a man, you see, and I don't want to abandon her just like that. I have my responsibilities, I simply can't behave like a child. But if she won't see reason, I don't know that I shall have much choice. You were wise to marry a Western girl. Women from our part of the world are so backward, don't you think?'

I don't know that I demurred effectively enough. But a fresh round of whisky helped to clear the air. The doorbell rang, Diana walked out and fetched an American couple into the room.

Salim promptly untied his apron; Pamela and I were introduced to the new entrants — Charlie and Mary. Jan nodded to both of them as if they were old friends. Diana set about her hostessly duties and I walked over to Mary and drew her into conversation.

Charlie had been posted to New Delhi on behalf of an American newspaper and Mary was pantingly looking forward to visiting 'the mystic orient' for the first time in her life. What did I think of India?

I smiled, not quite knowing whether the question was intended as a joke. But no, Mary insisted it was important to get to know what a place was like from the natives themselves, the people who had lived and were born there. Sounded plausible enough, so I thought I would return service as best I could.

'And what do you think of America, Mary?' I quizzed.

'Oh, it's a great place,' she replied, 'simply fantastic. Have you ever been to the States?'

'Only a few times,' I said, attempting to suppress the laughter which was bubbling inside me. 'But never for long enough to know it as well as you do.'

The arrow missed its target, Diana brought round the drinks and Salim came over with Charlie to join our profound exchanges. 'Sasthi is great writer,' Salim began, 'Mightiest Indian with pen, arbitrating wisdom.' There were no smiles on any face; I started to get a queasy feeling and noticed Pamela involved in a most intense dialogue with the Hungarian poet.

'Do you write books?' Charlie queried.

'Occasionally,' I replied.

'And do you write in *Hindu* or...?'

'I am afraid I have never heard of that language,' I cut in, irked in spite of myself.

'Then what language *do* you write in?' Charlie persisted.

'I try to use English as she is spoke in this country,' I replied.

Salim jumped to my defence. 'Sasthi being too much modest,' he began. 'All British critics make mention in many papers of greatness. God is died young is title, very marvellous book, talking about India.'

I couldn't figure out if this whole show was a craftily organized pantomime or not. I could never have invented a character like Salim for any of my novels; reality defied all efforts of imagination. Diana verged on a caricature of herself. And the Mary-Charlie axis threatened to swamp comprehension. I was beginning to feel that old uneasy sensation, as if I was not quite there but somewhere far away, listening in bodilessly. The drink was working itself into my system, the women in the room began to assume fresh vitality. Diana's lips appeared far more engrossing than the words which emerged from her mouth. Mary's breasts awoke tactile longings. If the lights were dim, and there was soft music in the background, I would have loved to squeeze the two New World women tight against my chest.

'You speak English very well,' Mary remarked, shattering my momentary refuge into fantasy.

'Yes I know,' I replied, unsmiling, 'and I'm surprised so many people here can actually understand me.' Mary made no response.

Charlie had joined Pamela and Jan by now, Diana was out of the room. Only Salim hung around like a droning fly. I pulled Mary aside and sat her down on the sofa. 'Look Mary, do you want me to tell you about India?'

'Oh yes, please,' she replied, her large blue eyes adoringly focussed on my face.

'Well,' I began, with the stern expression of an Emeritus professor, 'the most important thing to remember about Indians is that they are a deeply philosophical people.'

'Yes,' she interjected, 'I've been told that before.'

'And the single most important tenet in their philosophy,' I continued, ignoring her interruption, 'is that of the *Lingam*. You've heard of the School of *Lingam* Philosophy, of course?'

'Not really,' Mary answered, her face framed in an expression of doe-like wonder.

'*Lingam* is an ancient Sanskrit word meaning the male phallus. And it is absolutely essential to the understanding of the Indian psyche. Basically, the *lingam* philosophy asserts that worshipping the male phallus is the sole purpose and function of women. Now, without comprehending the full implications of this philosophy, you won't get anywhere in trying to figure out the Indian. Because in every sphere of life, the *lingam* is a dominant feature.'

'But how does the male phallus figure in politics? I mean Charlie is really a political reporter ... do you think?'

'That's just it. You see, India is not like any other country in the world. The effects of *lingam* philosophy are totally pervasive. Whether it is politics or the inter-relational dynamics of social exchange or even in Art, the pivotal point is always the *lingam*.'

'Do you mean that every single Indian is obsessed with sex?'

'No, no, no, you get me quite wrong. I wasn't talking of sex at all. That's the shallow Western way of looking at things. The *lingam* philosophy is far deeper, much more comprehensive than mere sex. The *lingam* is both a symbol of power and potency and an instrument. Now, you can use the instrument in whatever way you like, but if you forget the symbolic significance, you'll miss the whole subtle orientation of the Indian mind.'

'This is very interesting,' Mary said, 'I wonder if there are any books you could recommend ...'

'There you go again,' I cut in, 'in this sphere of higher philosophy, books are of no real use. Besides, you don't read Sanskrit, and the only books there are have not been translated into any other language. You see, the Indian conceptualization of the *lingam* is basically an experiential philosophy. You've got to experience to know, all the ancient *rishis* have emphasized this point again and again. Books and talk may help, but they can never be substitutes for the real thing — a direct contact with the instrument and the symbol.'

'Now really, you're not suggesting ...?'

'I'm doing nothing of the kind. I am merely trying to tell you that in order to understand the Indian mind you've got to rethink your whole frame of reference. For example, in temples and other holy places, you'll find women squatting over huge stone phalluses.'

'You mean, with the thing inside them?' Mary asked, her eyes sparkling in bewildered fascination.

'Oh yes, quite frequently,' I replied, still sternly repressing the urge to let the cat out of the bag.

I had lived long enough in the States to know that gullibility was an endemic social disease, especially among post-pubescent girls hipped on hash and Hermann Hesse. But to find the wife of a newspaper reporter infected with the same proclivity was a fresh experience. Of course I was to discover that the boot was on the other foot. The machinations of the occidental mind are no less insidious than those of the oriental. Seductions take place in many spheres in varied ways; frontal assault is not the only method of vanquishing a foe. Whether I could or could not have seduced Mary remains a matter of irritating conjecture, since I never got around to actually putting her to the test. But other more elaborate examinations were to follow, in which I was to fare less than gloriously.

Diana blew into the room at this moment and announced, 'Dinner is ready. Shall we go down?' We all nodded assent, with me hastily swilling down the last drops of whisky left in the glass. As we were about to leave the room, Pamela sidled up to me and whispered, 'Either these people are totally mad or else there is something terribly sinister about this whole lot.' I was puzzled by her remark and promptly put it aside as the product of an over-heated female imagination.

The dining room was as opulent as the room we had just left: glass chandeliers, large oak table, silver cutlery and cut glass tumblers. I would never have imagined such luxury in the house of a writer, short of best selling authors in America. 'The money must come from somewhere,' I reflected, 'and not merely from magazine articles either.'

Biriyani and Russian salad were served in large silver dishes; the red wine was chateau bottled. Diana supervised operations with supreme finesse, while Salim performed the triple functions of wine pourer, expositor on Indian culinary lore and putative host.

'I understand you're about to become a follower of the prophet Muhammad, Diana,' I said, by way of a lead.

'I don't really believe in any one religion,' she replied. 'One is as good as another.'

'Not in the eyes of the law, they aren't,' I retorted, hoping to draw her out on what Salim had told me.

'Well, if you are talking of our marriage, I really didn't mind either way. I was quite prepared to live with him. But since he insisted, we got married.'

'But isn't there a slight problem about bigamy?' I persisted.

'Salim seems to think there isn't. Muslim law allows four wives, and he's got only two so far.'

'Surely Diana,' Mary cut in, 'you don't approve of bigamy.'

'I prefer polyandry myself,' Pamela quipped. 'Nice to have a second helping, when the first one has flaked out.'

No one laughed, starch was in the air, creaking and oppressive. Diana launched into a lengthy diatribe on the obsolescence of the nuclear family, the need for free and open sexual relationships, the irrepressible male urge for variety etc. Jan was quiescent, moodily staring into his wine. Only Charlie was restive.

'Tell me, Sasthi,' the political reporter ventured, 'would you care to write for our paper?'

For a moment I was stupefied. Here was a man who had asked me if I wrote in Hindu only an hour ago and was quite obviously totally ignorant of my work. And yet he was making this fantastic request.

'What makes you think ...?' I began.

'Diana tells me you wrote a piece on Bangladesh for the *Guardian*. Well, I think that establishes your credentials firmly enough. And we could use pieces like that.'

'What do you mean, pieces like *that*?' I asked, somewhat testily.

'Well, you know,' Charlie explained, 'articles which give the other side of the story. The kind of thing that balances Indian propaganda.'

'You mean by lauding the atrocities of the West Pak Army?' I threw back.

'Not really. What I mean is that you as an Indian can talk with authority, people will believe you. And you can help to redress the balance.'

'Is that why you are going to India, to redress the balance?'

'Now, you mustn't take it like that, Sasthi. It's a simple matter of journalistic objectivity. And you're in an ideal position to do it. You know, our paper pays rather well. And I understand you're looking around for some journalistic assignments right now.'

I smiled, not knowing quite how to take such a blatant attempt at bribery. I was poor enough to wish to pick up a windfall but I had never managed to subserve what little conscience I still possessed. Diana steered the conversation away from the collision course on which it was set. The guests round the table set upon the food with solemn silence while I concentrated on draining the excellent wine down my gullet.

Over the next half hour, an incipient anger began to suppurate within me. After the wine came the brandy, punctuated by stories of Diana's exploits in the Congo, Biafra and elsewhere. An itinerant journalist she certainly was. But there was another part of her character which surfaced inadvertently due to a question from Mary.

'And how is — these days?' Mary asked. The name was an African one, and Diana tried to snuff out the query. But my curiosity was on the rampage by now. I felt as if I were in a kind of Wonderland, where the key back to reality eluded me. My insistence however finally broke down the evasive wall. It turned out that our African gentleman whose well-being Mary was querying had been a refugee from Biafra with whom Diana had cohabited for a while in this very house in London. And that was not all. There had been others, Jan being the earliest beneficiary in this long queue. Just as other people collect stamps, Diana collected refugees, distributing her largesse long enough for the issue to have ceased making the headlines.

I could hold myself no more. 'I don't know what kind of a house this is,' I shouted, getting up from the table, 'but it certainly doesn't agree with my constitution. I don't write for papers under dictation and I never will, even for a million dollars. So, Charlie boy, you can stuff your assignment up your arse for all I care. And as for you, my dear idiot, you are a witless pawn, eleven books in Bengali notwithstanding. And I hope to God I shall never have to set eyes on any of you again.'

With this, Pamela and I strode out of the room, collected our coats and emerged into the clean wholesome air of a Hampstead night. I pondered that I had never been one to search for CIA agents under every dining table, and I couldn't believe that even if they did exist they would go about their jobs with quite such grotesque crudity. But sinister they certainly were, and Pamela was right.

I never did find out what role Salim played in all this. But it couldn't have been a pleasant one.

7

Decline and Ascension

> We have seldom an opportunity of
> observing, either in active or speculative
> life, what effect may be produced, or
> what obstacles may be surmounted, by
> the force of a single mind, when it is
> inflexibly applied to the pursuit of a
> single object.
>
> EDWARD GIBBON

This is how it all began.

Long years ago I alighted upon Hampstead with the genuine
conviction that this was where ART lived. Cradled in the innocence
of a born philistine, I fancied that the doors of perception would
swing open by regular attendances at 'intellectual' public houses.
There weren't many guides around in those days and I had to compile
my own dossier, grading each of these hallowed institutions
according to both the number and the credentials of celebrities who
frequented them. I believe I was more assiduous than any secret
service agent in the rigour with which I undertook my nightly
peregrinations round the pubs in this area of London.

I kept a note of the number of times a minor artist had
condescended to throw nods in my direction, the frequency with
which a mini major writer had had drinks with me, and most
important of all the exact count of minutes spent in the company of
someone who had actually appeared on television or earned a
mention in the *New Statesman*'s 'London Diary'. It was a state of
mind, you might say. I had very little confidence in the world and its
ability to judge my true worth. So I wallowed in the belief that merit
by association was a valid concept. Sooner or later . . .

Millenniums later, this description of the young man I then was
sounds funny, cleverly self-deprecating perhaps. But alas, it was
grotesquely, painfully true. I had read a little, but not nearly enough;
I had written a tiny bit, all perfectly worthless. And to cap it all I was
doing a job which earned me a handsome salary but had nothing to
do with the 'Arts'. I wanted recognition, I wished to be considered

sensitive. The way I set about achieving my goal was to arse-lick those who had attained some measure of prominence in those spheres towards which I secretly and ardently aspired. I was eminently vulnerable.

One early evening, just over a decade ago, I was standing at the bar in The Roebuck on Pond Street, Hampstead. I had finished my first drink and was about to order my second when in walked Konrad. He was a big burly man with a name. He worked for the BBC, possessed a mellifluous voice and was constantly flying off to the ends of the world to do 'mood' pieces for both the wireless and one or other of the prestigious papers. I was on barely more than nodding terms with him.

So this particular evening, seeing the pub was deserted, I thought I would seize my chance and offer him a drink, in the hope that we would get to know each other better, and notch up a point or two in my ego stakes by having spoken with a well-known personage.

I said, 'What will you have, Konrad?'

'Oh,' he replied, mildly surprised to receive an offer of this kind from someone who was hardly even an acquaintance. But he was too much of a veteran to let that deter him. So he responded with apparent conviviality, 'That's jolly nice of you. Whisky please, with ice.'

I summoned the barmaid, with my heart pounding in joyful glee at having finally established that first thread of communication, albeit a tenuous one, with an eminence in the flesh. 'Two whiskies, please,' I ordered. As I did this, I noticed a flicker of disapproval flit across Konrad's brow. The next few minutes went by in silence, while the girl poured out the drinks. I couldn't think of anything to say, while the renowned celebrity was obviously in no mood to indulge in the usual pleasantries of pub encounters.

The drinks finally arrived. I paid, splashed some soda in my glass and raised it to my lips with, 'Cheers.'

Konrad said, 'Thanks,' and extended his hand in my direction. 'May I?'

I couldn't follow at first but in a moment it was clear that he was asking for my glass. Naturally, I handed it over to him, mildly curious about what was to come. Konrad put the glass down on the counter, picked up his own and poured its contents into mine. The accompanying words were, 'I *never* drink singles.' He then ordered two large whiskies, for which he paid, while I endeavoured to recover from the blow. The reader will get some idea of the price I was willing to pay for the favour of a mild collision with FAME when I say that I stood by and drank both my own whisky and the one Konrad bought me.

This was the man whose widow I was subsequently to marry.

Despite the snub, I continued to pursue Konrad's company. I now know that he was an intrinsically generous person. He had a temper, he was arrogant and he hated putting in time with losers. But he also had great charm, immense vitality and an insatiable curiosity about people, even the lowliest of them. After that first encounter, he always said, 'Hullo,' whenever I happened to be around and insisted on buying me large whiskies without reciprocation. Over the next three years we developed a mild rapport, even if it was laced with a gentle disdain on his side.

Once he invited me and a girl I was living with at the time back to his house. His wife Pamela, who had been present throughout the pub session, did not utter a word. He had bought a bottle of whisky and we drove back in our respective cars at closing time on a Saturday night. The front room was in chaos and Konrad added to it by wiping off all the papers which were sitting on the circular dining table onto the floor. He was a man of expansive gestures and his overture of hospitality consisted of ordering his wife to go into the kitchen and prepare some food, followed by a command to me, 'Go and make love to my wife.' Meanwhile, he had poured out four whiskies (large ones) and his right arm firmly encircled the woman with whom I was living in 'sin'.

I was ill-versed in the permissive ways of the Hampstead world in those days and my initial acquiescence in his scheme was prompted both by curiosity and by an eagerness to avoid being considered gauche and unemancipated. Though I was not over-pleased either with the peremptory manner in which Konrad was directing the show or with the idea that he was going to have my 'girl', the ego affront was mollified by the fact that a 'famous' man was doing it, that the evening's events would necessarily establish a closer bond between me and a BBC personality. Also, I was going to get something in exchange — his wife.

I knew that 'my girl' was all set to have it off with Konrad. I also knew that though I did not especially fancy his spouse, my discriminatory faculties were not all that sharp under the influence of alcohol and the pressure of such an extraordinary burden of events. The one factor which neither of us seemed to have considered was Pamela's possible response to sexual approaches from me.

So when I went into the kitchen and offered my services, only to receive a brusque, not to say mildly violent, rebuff from the lady of the house, my stretchable capacity to suffer humiliation instantly reached breaking point and snapped. I sprinted back to the sitting room, put on my coat and 'ordered' my girl to do the same. An exchange was an exchange, after all. Why should Konrad pleasure himself with my property, while Pamela would have nothing to do with me? With my paranoid predilections I sensed a conspiracy — I imagined that it was yet another attempt to puncture my ego and leave me high and dry. The two of them must have worked it out between them, I thought, Laclos with a doubly sadistic twist. Dangle the carrot in front of the little Indian twirp, keep him salivating until the heroic Konrad has finished the job and then with the fait accompli neatly sewn up, offer an anaemic, 'Sorry, old chap, never know women's whims, do you?' as an olive branch.

I strode out of the house in a mood which must have approximated closely to anger, dragging 'my girl' with me. The last visual image of that evening I can summon to mind is that of an inebriated Konrad swaying on his feet, brandishing a half-empty bottle of whisky in his fist, with words of uncontrollable fury shooting out into the still Hampstead night. As we turned the corner in the car, I saw Pamela emerge from the front door, take the bottle from his hand and lead her drunken husband like a child back into the house.

It took me years to realize that the 'whims' of women are not always whimsical. Of course the lady had been upset by Konrad's approaches towards 'my girl', but she had been thoroughly outraged by my impertinence in taking her for an exchangeable commodity. *Mea culpa, mea maxima culpa...*

Unbelievable as it may sound, the next time I met Konrad in the pub he did not mention the incident, nor did I. Alcoholic amnesia has its own devious ways of dealing with super-heated egos. He stood me a drink, I bought him one in return. We appeared to be 'friends'.

Several months afterwards, I invited him and his wife to a party I threw at 'my girl's flat. He accepted the invitation on condition it was *not* a bottle party. 'I hate lugging drinks around. If *you* throw a party, *you* provide the booze.' I assured him I would and he arrived punctiliously on time. His wife joined him later, having been involved in a minor car crash en route from her house. All the time Konrad was by himself, he was tense; his concern for Pamela was obvious and, to me, somewhat incongruous. When she did finally arrive, Konrad relaxed into his old jovial self again. At one stage in the evening, he had five women round him, lapping up every word he uttered and each gesture he made with a ravenous appetite. I felt a pang of jealousy of course, but there must have been a part of me which paid homage to a redoubtable charmer.

I talked with Pamela for a while, learned she was pregnant and that Konrad was flying off to Saigon in three weeks' time. When he joined us a few minutes later, I tossed off the remark, 'Watch out for those nasty Vietcong, Konrad. They are said to be the best snipers in the world. And if you get knocked off down there, I don't know too many people who would want to look after the baby your wife is about to produce.' I have not regretted any other statement I have made in my life more deeply.

A month after he left London, Konrad was dead. He was cremated in Saigon under instructions from his wife, and his ashes were flown back to London. Henrietta, the expected baby, was born a week before, but she never did get to open her eyes on the face of her father. I have often reflected on the insidious feminine psyche which named her after one of Konrad's erstwhile mistresses.

I met Pamela again some three years later in a Hampstead pub.

During those three years events of great moment befell me. At the time of the party, I had finished *My God Died Young*, hawked it around to some half a dozen publishers and had met with universally negative responses. The National Assistance people would have nothing to do with me any more — I had been living on the dole for over a year. 'My girl's patience was running out, since I was neither earning any money nor according her the status of a proper writer's mistress.

But there was one thing of which I was certain in my mind at this stage. Nothing would deter me from the goal I had set myself. I would emerge — however painfully — from a chrysalis, to become a fully fledged writer. There were others, manifestly less talented than I, who had 'arrived'. Why shouldn't I? I envied them their Oxbridge connections, their effortless ability to sit at the head of the table. I despised them for being in places where they had not earned the right to be. I was beginning to develop a subversive confidence in myself.

The relationship with my mistress was fragile at best. I was fond of her, we had great times in bed together. But I had upset the status quo with her family back in Yorkshire. She was getting on a bit, way past her mid thirties, and yet unmarried. A little fling with a coloured man some ten years previously might just have been tolerated. But with the vision of permanent spinsterhood looming large on the horizon, every year mis-spent was a further blow to the stocks on the marriage market. I was neither rich nor famous, and black into the bargain. An obviously unsuitable prospective husband.

Her own attitudes were sharply at variance, I must confess. But I was astigmatic enough to blame her for the hostility the family displayed towards me. I was recklessly unfaithful, and she knew it. This way I thought I would be getting my own back on those who had spurned me. More than an error of judgement there; rather a case of evil begetting evil, with the innocent go-between being pounded with pain. In all the years I spent with her, *I* never once thought of marriage.

Then the lights changed with electric alacrity. The book was accepted by a reputable British publisher. I received what to me then was a handsome advance in pounds sterling, to be followed swiftly by an unimaginable number of dollars from one of the biggest publishing houses in America. When the opus appeared on the stalls, every prominent critic in the English-speaking world devoted massive column inches to dissecting its merits and demerits. I had, finally, arrived.

I took off for America with my ego pumped to bursting point. For a year I roamed around under the delirious haze of an ineluctable success story. I appeared on television, aired my thoughts on the wireless; often I was accosted on the streets of Manhattan by admirers who sought my autograph. I wrote articles for handsomely paying journals, my photograph appeared in the *New York Times*. Women sprang up everywhere, pleading to be pleasured. The celluloid vision of a 'hero' came perilously close to fitting in with my own experience.

Then suddenly I fell in love. Her beauty had an ethereal quality, and her mind was equally insubstantial. More than anything else she reminds me now of that Bob Dylan lyric:

> *She takes just like a woman*
> *Yes she does*
> *She makes love just like a woman*
> *But she breaks just like a little girl*

I was hooked all the same. Within a month of moving in with her, I proposed marriage, seriously. A gesture which astounded me. I have often reflected on this and can find no easy answers. Never before had I thought of marriage other than in flippant, contemptuous terms. All the while I was floating about, begging for a meal here and a bed there, when holy matrimony would have provided the ideal security within which I could do my 'work', I had never given it a thought. But just when I was amply able to provide for myself, when I had no further need to be beholden to anyone else, I inclined to that very curtailment of my freedom which hitherto I had so jealously guarded. Perversity? Perhaps.

I homed back to England on the understanding that my Beatrice was to follow a couple of months later. Rocking on the waves of a new-found euphoria, I rented a plush flat in Hampstead, and set to work on my new novel with the fierce, innocent energy of a man in love. I severed all previous connections, though the occasional one-night stands continued to occur. When the stipulated two-month period elapsed and my beloved was nowhere in sight, I undertook a tentative search in the forest of my mind, only to discover tell-tale evidence which suggested that my commitment was not as firmly embedded in the rock of love as I had once thought — rather it was weakly implanted in the soft earth of infatuation.

My ego stood its ground however and I decided I was damned if I was going to let the bloody bitch ditch me. So, once more with feeling, I winged my way to the States, this time to be given the final, violent brush-off. It is hard to describe the condition of dazed somnambulance in which I spent those three weeks in New York over Christmas in 1969. Though I knew I was no longer in love with her, I resented my 'toy' being snatched away from me. However tenuous the link, there is always pain when it is cut off, especially when the other does the cutting.

I have said I had set myself the goal of achieving the status of a writer. But there was yet another one, that of having a HOME. And brutally, just when I had succeeded in my first objective, the second (apparently more easily attainable) had been plucked out of my hands. I wanted a wife, children, a house in which I could be 'happy' and prosperous. All those brittle dreams had been smashed in one blow. Another man, a tinsel world, had curtained off the delicious dolly who was to help fulfil my gossamer ambitions. Once more I was free, with nowhere to go.

I charged around the east coast of America with the frenzy of a spiked bull — Boston, Vermont, New Haven, the lot. Anyone would do, just about anything with a slit between the legs and the normative qualifications of a spouse. I don't remember how many quick and sordid affairs I had in those few weeks. Nor how many innocent females I devastated with the futile vehemence of a man who feels the world has done him wrong. There is no use apologizing in retrospect, for I don't recollect either the faces or the places. It was not even debauchery, but something far worse; the grotesque, inchoate hunger of the thwarted animal masticating every bit of raw meat.

At the end of that ride round the ring, I fell into the arms of an angel and collapsed. She wouldn't marry me, no. But she would give me comfort. Charged with the sublimated aspirations of exhaustion, I made love with her. Unwittingly, I gave her something which revived faith in her own womanhood; to me she gave the one inestimable gift I prized over many others — the capacity to believe in the possibility of a future.

When I returned to London, my wound still ached but the convalescence was progressing satisfactorily. The 'angel' joined me a month later. We spent three incandescent weeks together, unfettered by the cloying demands of commitment. My friends in Hampstead were felled by a swooning adulation; without a hint of docility, she resurrected the dominant male in me. In her company I visited Westminster Abbey, the Tower of London, and all those other places I would never have dreamt of going to before. We drove down to Wales, paid our homage to Dylan Thomas territory. The nights swam by, my bed was warm with a woman who knew tender giving. At the end of her stay I was nearly a man once more.

When she left I was desolate. But I knew I could face the world. It was in this mood I met Pamela in a pub that night, three days after I had seen my 'angel' off at the airport.

In a sense I was riding the crest of a wave. I had published a book, I had money, borrowed from my American publishers, and was working hard on my new novel. Pub companions were deferential, not to say obsequious. I was living in a luxury bachelor pad, with booze flowing. Impudent fifth columnists attempted, on occasion, to puncture my balloon. But I was leadenly insulated against such attacks by success with wine, women and literary fame.

My routine was tediously mechanical. I wrote for most of the morning and a part of the afternoon, went out on the hunt by seven in the evening, imbibed large quantities of alcohol, picked up a bird more often than not, wove my way back to the flat with her, indulged in an hour or two of gorgeous fornication, woke up rather later than ten in the morning, served her breakfast and gently but firmly gave her the boot. Freedom unlimited!

There were times of course when it didn't quite work out like that. The lonely deserted nights, when soaked in alcohol I would stagger out of a pub to find a 'couple' wending their way back home, those solitary nights were hard to bear. There is a double edge to freedom. When you can pick up whom you like when you like, there always comes a moment when you would rather be fettered, return home to a nagging mistress or a wife. The solace of a bond, however restrictive, is hard to replace. Especially when there is no inner strength, no capacity to stand on one's own. The religious rigour with which a pub man attends the shrine is born of desolation. Those with inexhaustible resources don't need such external reassurances. But then neither do bovine minds, perfectly satiated by chewing the cud of repetitious daily routine.

That first encounter with Pamela in the pub was like any other. I was standing at the bar by myself, sipping my early evening whisky. She walked in from the other side and I caught a glimpse of her in the mirror. My hunter's instincts were roused; I knew she had not remarried since Konrad's death and she was unescorted at the time. So I walked over and offered her a drink. After a moment's hesitation, she accepted, muttering some words about having to go back home for supper. We had several drinks; there was nothing particularly enticing about the conversation that I can remember. At the end of a two-hour session I suggested we go out to eat. Pamela agreed with the proviso that she would have to go back and tell the people upstairs in her flat to keep an ear open for the children. The meal was not a spectacular success as both of us had had a great deal to drink. She drove back to her flat and after a minimum of demur, we went to bed.

The only thing that struck me about her that evening was her insistence that I should get out of bed before the children woke up in the morning. Even after three years of widowhood, she was obviously not having a regular affair.

That first meal and bed together was followed within a week by another and yet another. Each time I left the flat before eight in the morning, so the children wouldn't know that I had spent the night with their mother. My own routine remained relatively unchanged. I continued to pay my regular homage to pubs, and sometimes Pamela would join me. I wouldn't say we started an affair, since she did not demand and I did not offer any assurances of fidelity. The only difference was that when and if I felt the need for a companion both in and out of bed, Pamela was willing. It was an ideal arrangement for me, though she may have had other ideas. I was in no mood to commit myself to anyone, having been so recently bruised. I continued to lacerate myself with thoughts of that bitch in New York; on some drunken nights I still felt that old venom rising turbulently within me. So the antidote was reckless bedding with a multitude of women.

I have only now come to realize that the urge towards frenzied seductions, especially if it is prompted by a newly-broken affair, has nothing to do with sensual sex. The search for a different face and a new body is not directly connected with the anticipation of physical pleasure in copulation. It is largely the chase that incites, since the mind is kept occupied by the demands of the game. If you miss a move, you might lose.

Fidelitrous sex, on the other hand, has exactly the opposite effect. If a one-night stand develops into an affair, there is no need to reseduce your mistress before every session. This might mean that physical sex itself becomes more rewarding, tender, as you gently explore the mysteries of her body. But your mind may wander into irksome territory, like a tongue insistently snaking back to the gum from where a tooth has been newly extracted. For real commitment is always impossible as long as the old hurt has not healed.

This may be a male viewpoint at the moment but I suspect in years to come, it will be shared by both sexes. Just now the ego battle is fought overtly by the man and implicitly by the woman. The distinction is not instinctive but largely the result of convention. When a new set of parameters is introduced (as it is beginning to be), we will find women getting as much of a kick in seducing a new man every night and then dumping him in the morning — instead of feeling low and sluttish, she will use such experiences to massage her bruised ego — as the man has been proverbially allowed to do. This may not be a desirable prognostication for malekind, but it will happen.

Over the next few weeks my liaison with Pamela did not alter its character. The children hardly ever intruded in our dealings with one another; by the time I met her in the evening, they were already in bed, and the baby-sitter problem did not arise because of the people living directly above the flat. I did of course meet the kids once in a while on a Saturday afternoon or Sunday lunch time. I ate a good deal more home cooked food than I had for some time. And a certain cosy feeling settled upon me. Away from the pub, there was another world, more ordered, less desolate, strung out with the veins of 'responsibility'. This was a contrast, since the cardinal precept in a pub man's life is that of being unmoored.

There was one crucial thing that did change however — the state of my bank account. I had rapidly exhausted the dollars I had borrowed. Then I finished the novel and received an advance from my British publishers, which was pitifully low in comparison with the generosity of the Americans. I was not earning any money from any other source and since I had no intention of taking on a regular job, the end of the financially viable road was threateningly in sight. Not that this worried me unduly. All my adult life I had never let the lack of money disturb my peace of mind. Something would always turn up, an assignment from one of the heavy papers, another advance from the publishers, or even a kindly benefactor who would give me a loan or make a gift. I had lived precariously for nearly five years; my world wasn't suddenly going to crash into bits. Of course I had borrowed a great deal, often with no prospect of repaying the loan. I had lived off women, justifying myself by the notion that I was an artist — a man who has the inalienable right to break all rules in the game. I was never ungenerous with money when I had it; when I was broke, I expected my friends to pay for me.

To what extent I was attracted to Pamela because she had money is a moot question and I shall try to answer it honestly. I am absolutely certain in my mind that if she had been a typist in an office, living with two children in a Council house flat, I might have had a quick fling with her, but I would never have let it blossom into an affair. The reason for this revulsion has less to do with money than with the mental accoutrements that money provides. As an alien, lacking the security of a stable English background, I have always been incorrigibly attracted by the trimmings of bourgeois life. Though I theoretically despise the middle-class ethos, personally I would never wish to belong to any other milieu. My first years in this country inoculated me permanently against the romance of the working class. It is easier to be a radical from top down than from bottom up. I prefer wine to best bitter, coq au vin to fish and chips. Conceptually, there are archetypal patterns in my mind which no amount of rational analysis will dislodge. As a coloured man, I cannot afford the luxury of slumming. Orwell never was mistaken for the genuine down and outs of Paris and London: the Eton stamp is unerasable. If I married a woman from the working class, there would be the serious risk that people might think that that was where I really belonged. Liberal declarations apart, this would be a positive disadvantage. But what if I fell desperately in love with a cockney lass? Would I let such superficial considerations of accent and money deter me from making her mine for life? These questions are rhetorical because it just wouldn't happen. My mind is too well-trained for such calamities to befall me. My resistance to particular social types is practically fool-proof. This may sound snobbish but it is the ugly face of a perennial anxiety; an inadequacy that every person who hails from the lower echelons of the social ladder possesses. For one Aneurin Bevan, there are ten thousand Evelyn Waughs.

Even when I have been extremely poor, I did not lose the confidence that one day I would be able to provide handsomely for myself, perhaps even for a family, out of my writing. My fortunes have fluctuated so wildly that neither the troughs nor the crests have left very much of an impression, except in the most superficial terms. All these attitudes made their mark on my relationship with Pamela, but I don't think money was one of them.

I must warn the reader at this stage that the foregoing pages may have been a deceitful device to lead the potential critic astray. My wife, who has read the account up to this point, thinks it is heavily loaded in my favour, with lies, omissions and other ego cosmetics thrown in — all with the intention of making everyone else in the drama look like a blackguard, while I emerge spotlessly pure, a worthy candidate for canonization. I do not defend myself against such attacks, I merely record.

Of course I went on drinking in pubs, but the frequency of these visits began to decline. And this in turn was bound to produce higher expectations of good behaviour. Previously, when I was certain to be drunk every weekend, it was assumed that this would be so and there were no complaints when it was. When, however, more and more weekends began to turn out wholesomely free from the Bacchanalian clutch, the odd weekend when I did go on a binge invited that much harsher judgement and censure.

Naturally, on such occasions confrontations were doomed to occur and the ensuing row would be mercilessly cruel on both sides. Necessarily, the haranguing would go on, maudlin, doused in self-pity, circular, hurtful and exploding with half-truths. And there would be the danger that history might repeat itself.

As a general diagnosis of this ailment, which must afflict a fair number of loving, middle-class households in this country, I might say that instead of treating it as a one-off aberration, the woman stakes her all in the combat, thus ensuring that that which she is seeking to prevent will indeed happen. When the pub man ought to be given a mild ticking off and treated like an errant child, he is taken for an adult and fought in earnest. When all he really wants is to try mama's patience, he is lashed with the whip, the screw's punishment for an escaped prisoner brought back within the iron gates. The prognosis for such treatment of the disease is only marginally more favourable than terminal cancer.

The above description of a general malaise may equally well be applied in the particular. Inevitably in a relationship there comes a point when fights occur. This might be the stage at which the scales of romance fall from the eyes and the whole thing flies apart at the seams. Or it may turn out to be the period of consolidation. It really depends how, when and why these confrontations occur. If they happen under the influence of alcohol, as they frequently did between Pamela and me, then with a dash of amnesia and remorse thrown in, the next morning may well find the two people somewhat closer together. The sober row is a killer. There is no way out for all those searing words and gruesome gestures. Trapped within the unforgetting and unforgiving mind, they suppurate. Fortunately for us, neither of us was ever totally uninebriated at the end of the day. So we survived. (Reader, please don't take this to be an open dictation to become generous donors to the distilleries of Britain and the vine-growers of France, for the preservation of marital bliss.)

As I have said, my life-style changed but Pamela's did not, except for one thing. Since I had dredged the bottom of the money barrel, and no fresh deliveries were about to take place, in slow, unobtrusive stages I began to become financially dependent upon her. I still had my flat, for which I went on owing rent; theoretically I maintained a separate establishment. But I ate most of my meals with Pamela, drank her booze. The only items I continued to provide for myself were cigarettes and the occasional drink in the pub — and that with money borrowed from a fellow writer. Either as a result of my precarious state or perhaps due to that old bogeyman called 'commitment', the habit of fidelity began to grow in me. If there were other women during that last lap of our liaison, before I finally moved in with Pamela and began to live with her, I don't remember much about them. Certainly, the reckless chase had been abandoned. It is also possible that my old hurt had nearly healed.

Then summer came and with it the thunder of devastation. I had at long last reached a stage when I had no money left. I was broke to the point of having to *ask* for half of bitter (which I never normally drink) at The Rosslyn Arms, and being unable to raise it, even from the landlord. Summer brings the school season to an end; children who have grandmas up in Yorkshire yearn to migrate; mothers, however reluctantly, follow suit and the great pilgrimage begins. And penniless geniuses who till then have been generously fed by those mothers face the unhealthy prospect of starvation.

But even at this stage I was proud. Though I was a pauper, I was sorely reluctant to ask Pamela for money. But I was scared too: for the first time in my life I was really tempted to give up the pen and turn into a gainfully employed law-abiding citizen. No more the hair-shirted young man who had said, 'Not for me the haute cuisine, I just want the raw meat.' By now I knew I had become addicted to certain aspects of good living. Did I still possess the nerve and the dare to ride it out?

The axes were clearly drawn. Pamela knew I was broke. I knew that she knew I was broke. But the knowledge was implied on both sides, never stated. Who then was to bell the cat?

This particular kind of problem has confronted me several times before, though never in the same crude and awesome manner. And despite the fact I may not have handled it right on this particular occasion, I think it deserves discussion. Simply put, the question is this: in an impasse, where neither the one nor the other is either in the right or in the wrong, who makes the first move?

There are issues of ego involved — who stands to lose or gain, why does such a situation come into being in the first place? Above all of course the thing hangs over your head, and there are no quiescent sabbaticals during which you can mull it over in your mind. The response, when it comes, is almost always instantaneous, though of course you have seen it zooming towards you for months. But that is poor consolation. You never do imagine that it is actually going to happen, you shut your eyes and hope it will go away. But it never does. Finally, the lemon is squeezed dry, the whistle blows and the train is about to leave the platform. And then,

> Should I, after tea and cakes and ices,
> Have the strength to force the moment to its crisis?

(Not the last reason why people write books, anyway.)

I reckoned I was an ARTIST. Therefore I had the right to. . . To do what? I didn't quite know. The dividing line is thin: how much self-indulgence and what degree of conviction? Writers, more than any other animal in the artistic menagerie, have often used their vocation as an excuse to perpetrate the most heinous deeds. How much of Tolstoy's cruelty towards his wife was the necessary concomitant to the greatness of his work? Was Balzac's vulgarity the plinth on which his huge tomes were built? Or do we subsequently psycho-theorize his inadequacies into the origin of his work because of a puritanical refusal to accept that genius may be blemished, split into compartments, some of which have nothing to do with the final work itself?

My attitude towards my own work oscillates wildly. There are days when I feel that I might have had a thing or two to teach that old bard, if I had lived at the time of Shakespeare. On other days, when the barometer reads low, I am equally firmly possessed by the nihilistic belief that the million or so words I have so far put down on paper might just as well have been thrown in the autumn bonfire, with no one being the loser. In general, the closer you get to your target the more humble you feel, the greater the chance that you will make a correct assessment of your work. Only during periods of infertility do the reckless claims get made, the incipient virus of folie de grandeur infects your system.

The day after Pamela left for Yorkshire with her two kids, I started a book. Four weeks and seventy thousand words later, I had finished the opus. I titled it *The Making of a Mystic President*. In the course of writing the book I must have been carried away by the arch aspirations of the hero. For not only did I imagine at the time that it would be published and wildly acclaimed by the whole of the English-speaking world. I was scripting imaginary scenarios in my mind for Foyles luncheons, international premières and Knighthood at the Palace. In the event, neither my British nor my American publishers wished to touch it with a bargepole. It was too hot to handle; not for them, they said, these exotic and spicy dishes. There was one scene which especially put them off. In the autobiography of the would-be President — a book within a book — there was a graphic description of a four-and-a-half-year-old boy fucking his mother with an eight-inch-long prick. It was more even than the libertarian instincts of two of the largest publishing houses in the Western world could stand. Little did they realize that I was riding my High Church literary horse in that particular chapter, for it was a satirical pastiche, a send-up of one of the most popular and eminent novelists in America.

During those four weeks, I had literally no money. I managed to scrounge a meal from the woman upstairs every so often, and borrowed a few bob to keep on a couple of halves a day. I worked between sixteen and eighteen hours out of every twenty-four. There was no question of inspiration, flashes of insight or any of that rubbish that outsiders always invoke with a solemn voice. I had not written for over four months. There was no other way I could pluck myself out of the well of morose despair into which I had fallen. My aim was to fell two birds with one pen. Money, and that singular lift I so badly needed to take me out of a near-suicidal depression.

Towards the end of those four exhausting weeks, two incidents occurred which jerked me out of the groove. I don't mean they brought about the change solely by their own impact but they certainly gave the final push and, to change the metaphor, made me fall off the razor's edge on which I had been precariously perched.

But before I go on to relate these two incidents, let me attempt to explain my creed, especially as it applies to autobiographical writing. To start first with the prosecution case, which, though it comes in different forms, is really an exasperated and outraged attack by the pleb on what he considers to be the Artist's superhuman ego: Do you have anything to say? Isn't it a lack of *imagination* which makes you churn out autobiography after autobiography? Why don't you write *proper* novels for a change? Is there any UNIVERSAL message to be discerned in your writing?

Apart from the abysmal level of intelligence these questions display, they also indicate a singular lack of understanding about what Art is. But since they have been so frequently hurled at me, and not always from uneminent quarters, I feel that this is as good a place as any to put them out of the way, once and for all.

To me the question of whether I have anything to say is a fatuous and irrelevant one. I firmly believe that everyone, but everyone, has something to say. If you can find out what is unique about yourself, discover that single element which makes you different from everyone else in the world, you have already performed a remarkable feat. If you can then express that part of yourself with direct sincerity in words, you are a writer. Whether people like you or not, they will be forced to listen. And at the end of the day, you will be remembered as a witness of your time, long after the pundits and critics and politicians have sunk deep into oblivion.

I believe that human experience in the latter half of this century is vastly more fragmented and discontinuous than in all the previous history of man. To take the omniscient stance of the nineteenth-century novelist is ludicrous in the present day. The only thing I know directly and for certain is my own life: the rest is intelligent conjecture or intuition at best. The minds of an astronaut and a pygmy in Africa are qualitatively apart. I cannot know either of them. My job as a writer is to say, this is what I am, this is what I experienced. And if my voice rings with authenticity the writing will be valid and worthy of a hearing. It may also act as a catalyst for change.

It is not *lack* of imagination which induces me not to write what some people call proper novels. It is because I find that the conventional novel form does not allow me to exercise the full range of my imagination that I eschew it.

Art must not be confused with the outpourings from a dictaphone machine. No so-called autobiographical novel, if it falls into the category of good Art, is a verbatim record of anything described within it. The selection of material, the rearranging of events, the background against which an episode is related — all these require the long active pressure of a fertile fancy in order to transmute the carbon of dry daily data into the diamond of ART.

The real artist is a magician; an obsessively autobiographical writer, if he is also a true artist, may be an invisible man. When you think you know him best, he may be being his most elusive. There are no clear-cut answers to any of the examiner's questions; the proof of the pudding is in the eating. Art is not a pursuit of Truth. Great Art happens when the attempt to capture Reality succeeds, even for a second, a page, a paragraph or just a line.

I do not normally cast around for a homeless UNIVERSAL message to come and abide with me in my study before I start work on a new book. In general I tend to avoid the company of such wholesome and righteous creatures.

When I write I like to dwell in those dark archives of my mind, which, while exuding their musty odours, tell me of another world and another me which is no more. And when I look at that me and listen to his voice, I sometimes feel that that face and that voice did not belong only to me but to many, many other people about whom I had read, whom I had heard, smelt and touched. And suddenly, if I am lucky, I am able to travel to many lands, visit many peoples and speak with many tongues.

In moments such as these I don't feel dejected about not carrying a UNIVERSAL message in my pocket. What I do is wink at myself in the mirror, draw up the chair to my desk, uncap my fountain pen and prepare to describe the two incidents about which I warned the reader, before I went off at a tangent.

The first happened in a pub and was innocuous enough at first glance. I was at the bar in The Washington, Hampstead, sipping my midday ration of half of bitter, when a tall man appeared by my side and ordered a round of drinks, including a pint of Guinness, in the New England accent. While waiting for his drinks, he turned sideways and threw me a polite, half-quizzical look. I returned his gesture with a smile.

Then he said, 'You look like a character out of the eighteenth century.'

To which I replied, 'And you look like Robert Lowell.'

He showed surprise and was inordinately, almost childishly pleased to be recognized in a pub. (Which goes to show that even the great have their Achilles heel.) With my obsessional penchant for hanging onto the coat-tails of celebrities, I invited myself to his table and was introduced to Elizabeth Hardwick and another American friend. The lady spotted me for the name collector I was and I suspect she also sensed my discomfiture. For having sat myself down at their table, I could not think of anything to say. Lowell and his party on the other hand must have been having an intimate conversation into which, obviously, I could not be easily introduced. Nor could they go on from where they had left off without violating the elementary rules of courteous behaviour. The result was that for the next five minutes a total void descended on the four of us, with three or four unsuccessful attempts from Elizabeth Hardwick to breach the silence.

At the end of that period of irksome non-communication, I leapt to my feet and announced, 'Mr. Lowell, I would like to give you a present. If you will care to wait for me, I will be back in ten minutes.'

Whatever they must have thought of me I don't know. But I was in no mood to care. For the very first time in my life, I had met a *great* man. And I wasn't going to let an opportunity like this go by. I had no venal motives, no hope of gain, mere association was enough. I sprinted off to my flat in Fellows Road, with my heart racing faster than my feet. I picked up a copy of *My God Died Young* and flew back to the pub with the speed of a man possessed.

They were still there, thank God! I sat down and said in the most whimperingly obsequious voice I have ever mustered, 'Will you please accept this humble gift from an ardent admirer, Mr. Lowell?'

He said, 'Of course, it will be a great pleasure. You must sign your name.'

Elizabeth Hardwick said, 'You must not be so modest, young man. I have heard of this book, I remember reading a review of it in the *New Yorker*, but I must confess I never did get around to reading it.' I had no words to reciprocate this effusion of generosity. 'Look me up when you come to New York next,' she said as a parting gesture. 'The number is under my husband's name.'

When the three of them left the pub, I sat there dazed. 'I've actually met Robert Lowell,' I went on incanting like a magic mantra. At closing time I had consumed three pints of bitter and was mildly inebriated. I went back to the flat and the sight of all those sheaves of paper and the typewriter did not make much of an appeal. So I set out in search of someone who would provide me with booze and on whom I could disgorge my glorious news. As it happened, I found just such a person in the form of a Canadian copy-writer who lived immediately above my flat. She had exactly the right combination of liquor in the house — a bottle of whisky and a little dry white wine. For the next four hours, we consumed all that alcohol, with me bagging the lion's share. By seven I was wildly drunk, while my lady-friend was only pleasantly merry.

In this mood of delirious intoxication, the two of us set out to the pub. As I entered The Washington, my eyes were assaulted by a sight which restored me to partial sobriety. For who should be sitting there at the same corner table but Robert Lowell himself, alone this time, sipping his pint of Guinness. I walked over to him, followed by my lady-friend. He rose from his seat and offered us both a drink. While he was at the bar, my mind rocketed off into the outer reaches of ego ecstasies. I had proved to my Canadian friend that I had indeed met the great man. Furthermore, he had recognized me and was buying us a drink. I searched for something to say, some startlingly witty and brilliant remark which would set the seal on our acquaintanceship. But it was a fruitless endeavour; I was too drunk to dig out any of those sparkling gems, even if they had been there at all. So I fell back, as I invariably do, on invective.

The psychology behind this mode of behaviour is not all that complicated, though the exact form of vitriolic aggression I display on such occasions says a few nasty things about my character. Generally, in any social encounter, I prefer to be abrasive rather than smoothly pleasant. But in the company of a celebrity, and under the strong influence of alcohol, this predilection reaches ludicrously tasteless heights. I reason that *most* people who meet a well-known person are prone to be obsequious and deferential. And since the celebrity must meet a lot of strangers, all such people who have only pleasant or flattering things to say, must be massed together in his mind, without any features distinguishing one from the others. In short, they are no longer individuals but fall under the collective label of 'adulators'. On my first meeting with Lowell at lunchtime I had been sober and had thus fallen a victim to this snare. In the evening, with massive help from Lord Bacchus, I was determined to make a mark, to be *different*, to be incisively insulting.

My memory is hazy about everything that happened at the second meeting. My lady-friend was more sober than I, and being unable to suffer the asinine spectacle I was making of myself, withdrew half way through the session. Lowell and I must have spent some two very boozy hours together. I understand I lashed out at him for displaying no social concern, for behaving like a coward by running away to England while America was burning. I accused him of having dried up because he had resorted to reworking other people's poems rather than writing his own. (I was referring to *Imitations*.) I went on to say that to take refuge under the quilt of mental illness was to shirk responsibility and practise a particularly noxious form of self-indulgence. I also asserted that I myself was shatteringly brilliant, that my books were under-recognized for the immortal works they were, and it was the sacred duty of anyone even remotely interested in English literature to have read every single word I had ever written etc. etc. etc.

Next morning, I woke up with a monstrous hangover and a strangulating feeling of guilt and lost opportunity which was bleakly suicidal. At half past eleven that same morning, I was summoned by a knock and there was Robert Lowell standing outside my front door. As I started to blubber an apology, he stayed my words with the comment, 'If you had not said those things, we would never have become friends. Now I feel we are.'

It should not be difficult to guess what effect those soothing words had on me.

What brought him to my flat I shall never know. For I never did ask and he did not venture to explain himself. During the course of the previous evening he had taken down my address, and it turned out that he was living literally next door, just a house away. So ... Over the next ten days, he made these morning visits regularly; it became an unspoken ritual. We would have coffee or go out for a drink. He knew I was broke, and often he would leave packets of cigarettes behind in the flat. There was little we talked about, and the small amount of conversation there was had nothing to do with literature, art or poetry. Mostly it would be an account of something that had happened the previous day, or about an encounter he had had with a Hampstead poet we both knew.

I can only speculate why this world-renowned man deigned to be involved with an insignificant scribbler like myself. Perhaps, at that moment in his life, he needed the company of a stranger. Perhaps, too, he relished the obvious unbounded pleasure I got from his company. He might also have derived some satisfaction out of the unabashed display of hero-adulation from a vibrant young man. What effect I had, what I may have given him, I can never tell. But I can describe the other side of the coin.

I have said I started writing the new novel as an exercise in survival, the only antidote to depression I could commandeer. But to start a project is not to finish it, especially in a condition of extreme penury backed by an inhospitable future. I doubt if I would have finished the book but for Robert Lowell's daily incursions into my life and routine at that time. He helped me, by his mere presence, to climb out of that deep well of dejection into which I had fallen. He may have been aware that he was having this effect on me. On the other hand, he may have been acting in a private tableau of which I had not even the faintest glimpse. Perhaps it was a combination of both these factors. The only positive thing he did was to praise a short story I had pressed upon him. Other than this one response, there was nothing he did or said which could be remotely considered as an act of psycho-therapeutic salvaging. I doubt too if he was aware of the abject emotional and psychological state I was in. Nevertheless that was the result of his action. Once again it was one of those events in my life which have so often snatched me back from the edge of the cliff.

The termination of this first phase in our relationship was marked by a strange episode which has never ceased to intrigue me. One morning when he came into my flat, Lowell announced he was leaving Hampstead next day to go and live in Chelsea. He had already spoken obliquely about the lady he was later to marry. Obviously he had suddenly found himself in love all over again and was experiencing some strain in resolving the tensions. His move to Chelsea seemed to me a happy omen and it was clear that he himself felt the same way. He said, 'Look Sasthi, I feel like celebrating and I want to take you out for dinner tonight.'

Of course I was overjoyed and flattered and accepted his invitation with alacrity.

He picked me up from the flat at seven and we took a taxi up to the top of Hampstead. Lowell said he knew a good French restaurant but had forgotten its name. So we walked up and down the road several times, hoping that one or other of the sign boards would jolt his memory into recognition. When a quarter of an hour's search failed to do just that, I suggested we go to a place I had previously used myself. He agreed.

Lowell's mood seemed buoyant, he was looking forward to living in Chelsea and later to teaching at Essex. Half way through the main course however, his face suddenly clouded over and he announced, apropos of nothing, 'I must leave, don't come with me. I want to be alone.' Then he got up and strode out of the restaurant.

Of course I was thoroughly bemused and tried to figure out what might have upset him. As the conversation had been totally innocuous, I did not come up with a clue. So I attributed it to 'poetic temperament' (that dreaded artistic privilege again), assumed it would blow over, and that he would return in a while. When I had finished the main course, the waiter removed the dishes and asked if I wanted any dessert. By now I was beginning to get seriously worried about the bill, and as it was only a quarter of an hour since he had left, I decided to order for myself in the hope of dragging out the time long enough for Lowell to come back and settle accounts. I dawdled over my pudding, then coffee and later the brandy. An hour later, I knew I would have to meet this one myself.

I racked my brain for the name of some kindly benefactor who might bail me out. But though I had some friends who would lend me a pound or two for dire necessities, there was no one who would be willing to foot a hefty bill in a French restaurant, especially as they all knew that I had been on my uppers for some time. By a stroke of providence, however, I still carried the cheque book from my now-defunct bank account in the inside breast pocket of my jacket. As the restaurateur knew me, he accepted my cheque without query.

That cheque was, alas, a good deal more lethal than the ordinary bouncing variety. Two weeks previously the bank had written to say that since my overdraft had been outstanding for nearly a year, they had contacted my publishers in America, the guarantors, who as agreed had reimbursed the amount of the loan. So, would I consider the account closed? In writing the cheque therefore I was not only issuing a promissory note which I could not honour (the run of the mill rubber cheque), but I was signing my name on an account I no longer possessed. In short, I was committing a fraud.

Of course the full implications of my action did not dawn on me at the time. But some four weeks later the Hampstead CID and the restaurateur between them drummed home the possible consequences in fiercely unambiguous terms. The police had gone to the bank, inspected the file on me, and convinced themselves that it was a straightforward case of fraud — a criminal offence punishable by imprisonment.

I wheedled myself out of the mess by pleading ignorance, misunderstanding, delays in postal deliveries etc. The police agreed to let the matter drop if I paid up. I promised I would and Pamela supplied the money.

I met Lowell several times after that but I never dared to quiz him about the incident. For I do believe that a real artist *is* a being apart and entitled to break rules which apply rigorously to mere mortals. But the moral of the story is that it can be jolly risky to get mixed up with a man madly inspired by the muse.

Within a week of Lowell's moving out of Hampstead, my electricity was cut off. And needless to say I had no money to pay the bill and have supplies reconnected. As my typewriter ran on a motor, I was not only deprived of light and heat, but my work was put out of gear as well. I was on the last lap of my book and though I was mentally and physically exhausted, I desperately wanted to finish it, to put the last full stop and feel all that tightly bound paper in my hand: the thrill of a job completed, the ecstasy of a baby delivered.

The only choice I had was to move into Pamela's flat (she had left me with a key) with the typewriter and a few clothes. I had been extremely reluctant to make this decision, though for the previous few months I was in effect living with her. Of course I had gone on owing rent for my flat, so I had a place I could call my own. But the actual removal of the typewriter from *my* desk was a solemn undertaking and one which had a symbolic significance for me. I did move however, and completed the book four days later.

I no longer knew what I expected from it. I was sure I had done a good job, I was pleased with it. But I was not quite so certain any more about those headlines and TV interviews. I had lived with the thing incessantly and intensely for a month, during which I had eaten little and slept less. I felt a sense of both exhilaration and post-coital exhaustion at the same time. All I wanted to do was to snuggle into bed with a warm female body and go off to sleep for several weeks. Of course I had neither the money nor the energy to go out looking for skirt and booze. And Pamela was not due back for another fortnight. So circumstances compelled me to open the few tins that had been left behind in her cupboard, stay in bed and watch the box the rest of the time.

One such evening the bell rang at Pamela's flat and there was a friend of hers at the door. I had met the woman twice before and asked her to come in. She was obviously in a state and wanted to talk to someone, preferably a friend. Since I knew something of her condition, it was not difficult to persuade her to unburden. And the story was this.

She had come home from work to find the man she was living with, whom I knew to be an alcoholic, ruinously drunk. And the first thing he asked for was money to go to the pub. She had refused, they had had an awful row, he had threatened all kinds of silly things, and finally when she couldn't stand it any more, she had run out of the flat, partly to cool herself down, but largely to find Pamela who might be able to bring her man back to his senses.

The situation had occurred before. On one occasion she had come to Pamela in a similar condition and since I was in the flat at the time, the three of us had set out and tracked our man down in a pub. I had bought a round of drinks and sat down. The man started chatting quite soberly with Pamela, pointedly ignoring his girl-friend. But before I had had time to finish my single whisky, the man had collapsed onto the floor. He had barely drunk half a pint of Guinness in our company. We had then carried him to the car, leaving his mistress to drive him home.

The next time she had arrived, manifestly exhausted by his demands, and had asked Pamela to put her up for the night. On that occasion our man had been left to his own devices. And this was the third time round. But before I relate what happened that evening, I must say something about the man who occupies the centre of the stage in this episode. I shall call him David.

Though I didn't know him at all, the man intrigued me because we shared several frightening likenesses both in our careers and in our characters. David's association with Pamela was of twenty years' standing and he had seen her through many a difficult spot. She loved him as a friend and a kind of guardian angel. When his alcoholism began to get seriously out of hand, Pamela reckoned she owed it to him to give whatever help she could.

David was born a Welsh Methodist and always nurtured a nascent spiritualism. He had converted to Judaism in his early thirties. Though the background is similar, I do not yet know whether I shall ever take to any institutionalized religion. But having spotted some disturbingly mystical streaks in my nature, I cannot rule out the possibility. Then David went to University and from there settled into a satisfying but unglamorous teaching career. But after some years of student prodding, the urge to become famous and successful in the worldly sense overtook him. The same insistent hankering I feel for tinsel glitter and shallow accolade seems to have infected him somewhat later in life. As a personality he was witty, charming, well-read, full of vitality and always eager to hold the floor in any conversation. Most of these things have been said about me by friends. He also had a way with women. The darker side of the coin was of course a facility to switch sharply from elation to despair, those bleak periods of taciturnity. And the burden of guilt bore heavily down upon him. To my cost I know I share these traits.

After this, his career came to a crossroads which I have not yet reached. David joined the flamboyant world of television. Though he did not appear on the screen, he was a power behind it, and the job paid handsomely. As part of his new social image, he began to drink, at first moderately, then more and more heavily. The slide down the hill had begun and it was only a matter of time before he would be sacked from his job — after, of course, he had been given several warnings. For months he refused to admit that he was an alcoholic and intead of attempting to cure his addiction with medical help, he went around looking for another job. And the more frequently he failed, the more despondent he grew, and the more he drank. After the golden-handshake money ran out, his mistress began supporting him, and that added a new and intolerable burden, which further goaded him towards that final point of no return.

Now, I shouldn't carry the parallel too far, for I am a fair distance away from being a confirmed alcoholic. But drink *is* a problem for me and for not very dissimilar reasons. In a state of stress I always turn to alcohol for refuge. Almost all my relationships to date have broken up, directly and indirectly because of drink. Even on social occasions, with a large amount inside me, I am liable to be something of an embarrassment. The difference between addiction to the pub and to the substance that is consumed inside it is probably only a matter of degree. Though I have not yet become a secret or solitary drinker. Nor do I pass out on half a pint of Guinness. Yet!

David was finally persuaded to accept his condition and take a 'cure'. And it was then, in a way, that the tribulations really began for his mistress. For a cure offers *hope* both to the patient and those who are closest to him, when the prognosis for a far-gone alcoholic is pretty well certain disaster. The cure is a postponement of the inevitable, the suffering is most intense for those whose hopes are repeatedly resurrected only to be buried again a few days later. During those periods of sobriety, which become progressively shorter, between the end of one drying-out session and another relapse, the tension reaches breaking point. For in addition to the constant dread of finding a drunken David in her flat at the end of the day, the mistress had to put up with the wiles of a pathologically distorted mind. He would say he had written and sold a play to a television company when in fact he had just typed one line. The incessant need to doubt every word, every gesture, to treat her man like a delinquent child — that sort of pressure is agonizingly hard to bear, especially when in your core you know there will never ever be good times again, when there is no real chance of recovery. David's mistress could not abandon him and make a separate life for herself, because of that feminine propensity for responsibility and guilt. Nor could she get *any* of the things that a relationship normally provides. For in an alcoholic, even feelings become grotesque distortions of the things they once were. It is like living with a beastly mutant whose ancestors were once human, except that the mutation takes place under one's very eyes in slow but inexorable stages.

How far the parallel extends between David's personality and mine, it is hard for me to assert precisely. And whether I am on the same road, going to the same place, only time will tell. But there were enough points of correspondence for me to dread the man even as a concept, for I had hardly spent even five minutes in his company.

So when David's mistress came to Pamela's flat that evening, I was both morbidly curious and achingly nervous. My first suggestion was that we immediatey get in touch with him on the phone. If he was as drunk as she said he was, he might actually do something silly. So she tried several times to get him on the blower but there was no reply. And she interpreted this by saying that he *had* gone out to the pubs in the hope of getting credit somewhere. Contrary to my speculations, which were that, as he had just had a row, he was sitting there and sulking and deliberately not answering the phone. Or alternatively he had passed out.

So she strove out in her car, confirmed in the certainty that pubs were where to search for him. I did not share this certainty, nor was I that confirmed. But she drove a Volkswagen and I had no money. So, as in many other situations, I acquiesced. We ran around some sixteen pubs in N.W.1 without having a drink in any of them (much to my thirsty discomfort, I might add, since I had not had one for over a week). The total amount of time consumed in this wild peregrinating activity was something in the region of twenty minutes. After this tour of the reputable boozing houses in the area, I insisted that the lady driver lead us to his/her abode. She was reluctant at first, but after a little persuasion she relented.

She drove to the front of her flat, which was on the top of a four-storeyed house, and we could see from the street that the lights were on. 'Oh God,' she cried.

'No call to summon the Almighty,' I replied flippantly, hoping to introduce a note of relief. 'He is still there, as I said he would be.'

'I hope you're right,' she replied breathlessly, turning the key in the door, and we started racing up those indomitable stairs.

At the top, hanging from an intruding ledge on the window sill, was a rope. At the end of that rope was a man. David! Swinging! DEAD!

His mistress cried, 'Oh God,' and ran hysterically down the stairs. I was alone, and there was this man ... His left foot was still entangled in the steps of the small ladder with which he had hoisted himself to that position. He had obviously changed his mind at some point. But by then it was too late. So he had failed.

I bashed in a window, got hold of a piece of glass, climbed up to the top of the step-ladder and cut the rope. The corpse fell thud on the landing. A few minutes later, several well-meaning Samaritans, excluding his mistress of course, arrived on the scene, and I was informed with doctorial assurance that the 'man' was dead.

I felt him and he was still warm. I was no medical expert, but I was certain that if he really had done the bunk, it couldn't have been centuries ago. All those pub tours ...?

My response to calamity is always antiseptic. I react later.

I called the ambulance, got in touch with *her* friends and waited.

Somewhat stunned, I must confess, but still in full possession of my senses. David's mistress was in a flat into which she had been invited. When I knocked on the door, I almost had to seek permission to enter. Some twenty minutes later her friends arrived (before the police and the ambulance) and drove her away. I stood there on the pavement, feeling sordid and de trop. I suppose she was too shocked to say 'thank you' or even a 'goodbye' to me.

That night is the nearest I have come to losing my mind completely.

I roamed back to Pamela's flat, in a state I shall leave the reader to guess. There was no drink in the house, it was past pub time, so I woke up the landlord. Kindly and considerate as all such Hampstead liberals always are, he stood me a whisky and listened to my tale. Apropos of nothing, I told him I had taken LSD and seen a dead man hanging on a rope. He threatened eviction and I collected my faculties securely enough to inform him that neither of those two activities, since they were both in the past tense, constituted a crime against the law of the land.

It was one thirty in the morning. I clambered down the stairs, got into the flat and dialled Pamela's mother's number in Yorkshire. The old lady answered the phone, and after making her displeasure unambiguously clear, put her daughter on the line. I don't remember what I said to her, but Pamela tells me that I pleaded with her to come back to London instantly. I might have done. I don't know. And I certainly don't regret it if I did.

Next day she came down from Yorkshire with her two kids, and we were off to Cornwall the next day.

That of course was the lift-off and the rupture. For the first time in my life I had appealed for help, helplessly. And Pamela responded. She didn't say much but implied a lot. Like a good Yorkshire lass, she cloaked her offer in ungaudy colours. 'You need a holiday, Sasthi. Let's go off somewhere.' I assumed that the whole gesture was made for me, and as usual I was egotistically pleased, momentarily forgetting all my other worries.

When we got to Cornwall, the worm began to turn. I realized that Penzance had been chosen because it was on the sea and the children could go splashing in the water all day. And of course somebody had to be with them, since there were no baby-sitters or nannies around. We were living in a ten by twelve caravan, so that even love-making at night became an irksome activity. I was no longer the sole focus of her life; Pamela had other things to worry about. And this realization hit me just at the time when I could do with a bit of solace.

I resented and hated her. I felt cheated. There is nothing more infuriating to a single man than to have to put up with the futile drudgeries of progenital life. I would have preferred to have stayed on in London and suffered, rather than undergo this humiliation, this degrading dependence upon the inconsolable habits of two brats. I raged and shouted; with the fury of financial impotence, I declared I would fly back the coming day.

During those two weeks, I came closer to the two girls than I had ever been before. Though the situation was imposed upon me, and despite the fact I chafed inwardly, my reactions to the children were amazingly affectionate. Even adult love is easier to put down in words than the burbling cauldron of feelings one has for a child. So I shall not attempt it. Suffice it to say that in Cornwall I came to the conclusion that I could *live* with this family. Even though I reckoned that Pamela had cheated me into thinking that this was going to be *my* holiday, when in actual fact I was tagging along as an undeclared and unpaid au pair, with certain extra perks from the mistress of the house.

When we returned from Cornwall, it was unofficially accepted that I had changed my residence. A new stage in my life had begun.

It is difficult to carry the narrative forward from this point on without lapsing into abysmal sentiment or alternatively adopting a starchy attitude which would reveal nothing. I can say I began to love the two girls very much, perhaps in a way more obsessively than even their mother did. For I had missed family life in the last twelve years and I was overwhelmed by the load of affection that was showered on me. The 'little one' especially got me. I know this document is going to be read by both the children and their mother, but I can't help telling the truth. I enjoyed Pamela's company, of course, but I had responded equally vigorously to several other women in my life before. The children made the difference, a substantial one. Specifically the little one. The older one went to school, while Henrietta didn't. I had her in my bed for most of each morning. Call it the Electra complex if you like. We certainly developed an understanding. She was no different to me than if she were a product of my loins. I loved her intensely.

I was still very poor, I was not writing but I was being fed and loved. That made a lot of difference. In a short time I had regained my confidence and vitality. Two months after I had moved in with Pamela, I applied for a job advertised in the *New Statesman* and got it. They were going to pay well; I guessed I would get on with the group who were to run the magazine. I meant to leave myself a lot of free time and have a jolly good spree. In all these aspirations I succeeded. I was off again.

I must interrupt the flow here and declare that I have never really had a 'job' in the entire course of my terrestrial existence. I am now in the fourth decade of my life and I have never been *responsibly* employed. Everything I have done to earn money has been a kind of joke. I have either made fun of the people I worked for (inwardly) or, more importantly, I have made fun of myself. I can never treat the business of earning a living with any seriousness at all. This is not because I could afford to do without the hard stuff, quite the contrary. I just find the whole thing excruciatingly tedious and undeserving of critical attention.

When I started work for the magazine, the editor was three years younger than I and earning twice as much. I found this egotistically irksome but I also responded to the situation with a degree of surrealistic mirth. I genuinely felt it was hilarious that it should be so. Within a week of joining the staff, I contrived to arrange a schedule for myself which would leave me large numbers of unoccupied hours for boozing, writing or sheer metaphysical speculation. I did my work three times as fast as anyone else around and I reckoned I deserved the rest of the time to myself. So I would go into the office near about midday and invariably stride out by four in the afternoon. Unless of course I had been inveigled into staying till pub-opening time. No one in the office could write as well as I did. So I really faced no devastating competition.

Meanwhile of course my novel had gone to press and was scheduled for publication a few months ahead. At the page proof stage (a fairly advanced point in the production of a hardback book), I was imperiously summoned by the head of the publishing house and told to *cut* some fifty pages, out of a total of three hundred. I experienced the usual shock but more than ever my internal laughing machine was operating on full steam. I told the learned gentleman that I would do all at his behest but *cut* those pages I would not. There then followed some lengthy correspondence (which I have scrupulously preserved for posterity and the British Museum) in which I was asked to extract the word referring to the female genital *five* times in order that I be allowed to retain it *four* times. I was also informed that Moral Infamy and the like were my comfort bearers, and for the sake of the preservation of the human species would I not consider ...? You can only laugh so long and no longer. I relented. At the end of the day, some three and a half pages were taken out in the final printed version. Though to what momentous moral upliftment such an action contributed, I shall never know.

Then on the morning of 31st December, 1970, the Editor announced that the company which owned the magazine had gone into liquidation; the journal was folding up as of that minute. We were all out of a job. But unlike me, everyone else had seen it coming and made provisions. I was out on a limb once again, without even the consoling solace of three months' severance pay in the bank. I tried to stir it up a bit by threatening to take court action, writing to the *Guardian* et al. but all to no avail. Liquidation was liquidation. Preferential creditors would be paid from existing assets, but staff members could go jump in the Thames for all they cared. Not surprisingly, the management didn't do too badly out of it all. They stayed out of work till the beginning of the next financial year, and, given their hefty salaries, received a handsome rebate cheque from the Revenue man. In a capitalist society, to him who hath more shall be given, from him who hath not even that which he hath shall be taken away.

We held a party at Pamela's flat that night. The Editor came with his wife, and so did a few other members of the staff. It might have appeared to them that we were affluent enough to shrug off the loss of my job. But appearances as usual were deceptive. I have never quite managed to *look* penurious. Even in the direst strait, I am said to exude 'a sense of prosperity'. Whether this helps or not I cannot say. I do know however that on that New Year's Eve night, there were several influential people in the party — television producers, editors, literary critics and the like. And yet my pleas for help fell universally on deaf ears. Except for one or two solitary and special exceptions, no one has ever helped me get a job or any other form of financial remuneration.

There was still a bit of money left and I went on one of the most intense and extended boozing binges in which I have ever indulged. Days coagulated, gelatinous, undifferentiated. A haze of alcohol blurred my vision and screened off my memory. I moved around like a zombie, not knowing what I had done to whom and when. There was that gnawing pain once again, no money, no job and no vision of a new book. Once more I was empty and infertile, and I leant heavily on Pamela, hoping she would recharge me. In states such as this, the sharpest accusations come from within oneself. The atmosphere is highly combustible, charged with that inflammable vapour of guilt, recrimination, self-pity and a dash of martyrdom. All it takes is the smallest spark, the merest hint of hostility, and the whole thing explodes into a conflagration of merciless and devouring proportions.

Thus it came to pass, some two weeks into the New Year, one Friday I started drinking at ten in the morning. Pamela said nothing but showed her disapproval by taking refuge in a sullen and sulky silence. When I could bear such unspoken oppression no more, I strode out to the pub. Amazingly, she joined me a while later. And if my recollection serves me right, she kept me company all through that day, with short periods of respite during which she performed the housewifely chores, cooked the children's supper, put them to bed etc.

By early evening, I was wildly and raucously drunk; Pamela too was inebriated, though she didn't show it as much. In any case I was hardly in a state to observe. I had not eaten anything the whole day, and I was in no mood to stop imbibing. I am told I turned down several offers of a meal and snacks. At the end of the pub evening (eleven o'clock at night) I had drunk enough to have regained partial sobriety. My walk was steady, my speech unslurred, though my pupils must have been dilated and my breath would have blown a breathalyser spring green.

It was at this stage, with Pamela still faithfully by my side, that I felt an overwhelming desire for 'some stimulating conversation'. So I invited a few friends back to our place, with a bottle of whisky and some wine to keep us company. Back in the flat, Pamela cooked a meal which my friends ate and which I naturally spurned. I was hungering after 'food for the mind', not for that vulgar adjunct to my body called 'the belly'. And the highland brew helped to quell any subversive longings in the latter sphere. At about two in the morning, Pamela adjourned to bed, while my two friends and I were still involved in an intense discussion about the spinsterishness of Morgan Forster's writing.

Some two hours later, while I was still panting hot foot after the most demure damsel of Eng Lit, one of the august gentlemen in the company collapsed on the sofa and fell into a totally unliterary slumber. Just when I was getting into my stride, the audience had been tragically reduced by half. But I was in a valiant mood, I would not surrender battle, even if there was only one survivor ... To my great good fortune, the remaining combatant in the field rose triumphantly to the occasion and we continued our aesthetic duel till about six in the morning, all the while sliding inconspicuously down the slopes of Glen Fiddich.

I could not have been too sober when my friend, an erstwhile protégé of Mr. Forster, left the house.

Such however are the mysterious ways in which the mystic mind machinates, that I was not yet sated. So I burst into the bedroom and woke up Pamela, asking, indeed demanding, that she opine on *A Room With A View*. Not unnaturally, she queried, through sleep-sodden eyes, 'Which room?'

This threw me into the most violent of tempers. Here I was on a pristine artistic quest, with all my faculties in full sail, when what should I encounter? An ignorant female, half-marinaded in whisky and the rest of her faculties subversively subdued by fatigue. I launched into a tirade, effusively decorated with the most scorching abuse. I understand that this metaphysical monologue lasted for nearly an hour, at the end of which I declared that I should never wish to set eyes on her again. Then I flew out of the room, banging the door explosively shut behind me.

From this point on my memory is crystal clear, as if I had never touched a drop. (Amazing that, when you come to think of it. The filtering mechanics of the human mind are truly astounding. Why some things and not others, why this moment and not ...?)

I gave myself little time. In five minutes, I opened the door again (not gently, dear reader, not gently), as if I was Henry VIII striding in. I stood there for a moment, waiting for Pamela to open her eyes and look at me. Then I shouted, 'Why don't you marry me?'

She blinked, smiled a very small smile, and replied, 'Will you repeat that?'

'I want us to get married.' My voice was more subdued by now. I would suspect almost tender. 'Will you?'

She smiled again, this time a little more openly, 'If you really want to.'

'Today?'

'If that's what you want.'

'I do.'

'Then you had better arrange it, hadn't you?' With this she turned her back to me in bed and pulled the covers over her face. 'Switch off the light, will you?'

I came out of the room, a good deal less stridently I might add, and poured myself a whisky. I registered the baritone notes emanating from those nostrils on the sofa. They should have deterred me, I quite realize, but alas snoring has exactly the opposite effect. Instead of quietening me down, those sonorous sounds spurred me on. At the end of the whisky and one cigarette, I had made up my mind.

I woke up the children and sought their permission. (Strange thing for an adult to do?) I had decided in advance that if *they* gave me their blessing, it would happen, frightening, absurd, and unlikely as it might have seemed, even to me, some twenty-four hours before.

I talked with Susannah and Henrietta for an hour. It was near about their waking-up time, eight o'clock. So they were not particularly grumpy. I explained what it would imply, I did not spare them descriptions of the possible unpleasant repercussions on their lives. The response I got was unequivocal. Both the children climbed out of their beds and in turn hugged me hard and long and chorused, 'I want you to be my daddy.'

With this gold-chip insurance policy securely tucked inside my emotional pocket, I entered the sacred shrine again and whispered (knowing Pamela was still awake), 'They've agreed. It's all settled. We're going to get married today.'

'How?' she asked, her voice scarcely above a murmur.

'Shall I switch on the light and tell you, then?' I queried.

'For heaven's sake,' she screamed, 'is this some kind of a ghastly game? What do you think you're playing at?' There were sobs in her throat.

I let those few dramatic seconds go by and then switched on the light. 'No game at all. Serious. Really.'

'Oh darling,' Pamela said, then turned her face away from me and started crying.

I stood there, immobile, feeling a charlatan, yet knowing I was not. For several long minutes nothing happened. It was a tableau, like one of those things we had done at school.

Then she turned round, got up from bed, nude, and came towards me almost threateningly. 'All right then, what are you going to do now?' No kiss, no hug, just that demonic look.

'You don't believe me, do you?'

'No, I don't. You've got to show me.'

'I've asked the children,' I pleaded.

'Really?'

'Yes I have, I really have.'

Pamela screamed, 'I heard you. They're in the next room, you know. And you have no right to do that. You can do what you want with me. But leave them alone, will you, leave them alone.' Then she switched off the light and jumped into bed, sobbing.

I stood there in the dark, not sobbing, but feeling intensely alone for a whole minute. Then I said, 'I am going to make a telephone call. You had better stay up for this one, I wouldn't wish you to think I was lying.'

There was no reply. So I did what I knew I had to do. I switched on the light, picked up the directory and, sitting on her bed, dialled Hampstead Town Hall.

It was then that my ordeal began. I was in a 'now or never' mood and would brook no postponement, no opposition. The man in the Town Hall insisted adamantly that ten days was the minimum period over which an application for marriage could be processed. So I banged down the phone on him. Then I tried several local churches at random: Catholic, Unitarian, Baptist, anything would do, provided they agreed to perform the ceremony that very day. But each of the holy men I spoke to declared unequivocally that a minimum time lag varying between three and five weeks would be necessary to go through the required rituals — putting up the banns and all the rest of that pantomime. So once again I had come into a cul de sac. I knew too that if it did not happen then, in all probability it would not happen ever, not between us anyway.

But there was one faint whisper of hope which came through the voice of an Anglican vicar I had rung up. He said that though he himself was powerless to help me in my mission, there *were* certain circumstances in which a 'special dispensation' could be obtained from the office of the Archbishop. But the circumstances would have to be very special indeed, and in any case, seeing it was Saturday, it was extremely unlikely that the office would be open.

As there were no avenues left to explore, I thought I would try this one for all it was worth, as a last-ditch effort. I invented the 'special circumstances' by concocting a story about having to leave on Monday morning on a hazardous journalistic mission to Tel Aviv. And since I had been 'living with' the person I wanted to marry for the past year, we both wished to make an 'honest woman' out of her before or if something were to happen to me. With this story well rehearsed, I rang up Lambeth Palace.

The response was disappointing — His Grace was not in London. But once again there was a crack in the armour of officialdom. The man I spoke to was sufficiently taken in by the urgency of my voice to reveal that the Primate of All England was in Canterbury at that very moment. He gave me a number I might try, though he wasn't very confident that anything would come of it. Sorry, that was the best he could do.

Since I had nothing to lose, I dialled the number and by one of those preposterous freaks of coincidence, I got the old man himself directly on the line. His Grace listened to me for a couple of minutes and then put me on to one of his minions. I repeated my story and the gentleman said, Yes, His Grace had granted permission and I would be able to obtain 'special dispensation' from the Westminster Sanctuary if I went there accompanied by my local Anglican vicar: he would ensure that the requisite papers were ready.

So I got back to the priest who had put me on this trail in the first place and narrated the developments. He asked us to come over and have a chat, as I had never before set eyes on the man. When Pamela and I arrived at the vicarage, the vicar's wife said her husband was in the church and would be back in half an hour. Meanwhile, time was running out; it was perilously close to midday, the zero hour at which the Sanctuary would shut shop.

To bring this thrilling story to a swift conclusion, let me say that the dear Vicar of St. Saviour's Church, Hampstead, arrived shortly afterwards, telephoned the Archbishop's office to confirm that what I had said was true, and accompanied us to the Westminster Sanctuary, where the Clerk had specially kept the office open for us later than the prescribed hour. We got our licence, asked the Reverend Vicar to include a sermon ('How can one have a wedding *without* a sermon?' I had replied, when asked if I would like one, at a little extra cost of course.) I also insisted that the organist play, 'Lead kindly light amidst the encircling gloom ...' instead of the Wedding March.

I continued to drink throughout the day and there was a particularly hectic but fruitless search for an Onyx wedding ring. At the last minute we settled on a gold one instead. So, at five o'clock, on Saturday, 16th January 1971, I waited at the altar in the church, with Richard Walsh, my best man. I was attired in a three-piece Savile Row suit, while Pamela wore a long scarlet silk dress. The congregation of twenty or so consisted mostly of children under ten, as we didn't have much time to get in touch with many friends.

And thus they were married!

The Vicar turned out to be quite a character with a pungent sense of humour. In his sermon he declaimed, 'Where the spirit moves, you must follow' apparently commenting on the impromptu nature of the wedding. But I am sure the smell of whisky on my breath did not elude him. Later when he joined us for a glass of champagne in the flat, he explained that he was a fully qualified *exorciser of Devils*.

There was a lot of talk in Hampstead about my sudden leap into the holy state of matrimony. The *Evening Standard* (London) described it as an 'Ecumenical Wedding', where a Jew 'gave away' an atheist who was married to a Hindu whose best man was a Christian, all within the precincts of an Anglican High Church. The 'Ham & High' put it somewhat more dully: 'Engaged at nine a.m. and married at five p.m.'

Evil tongues chattered of course. Some declared it was a publicity stunt for my forthcoming book. Others divined that it was a histrionic display in keeping with my adolescent character, and would not last longer than a few weeks. But three years later, as I write these words, my marriage seems to have weathered as well as I had ever hoped it would.

Six months after we got married, Pamela and I bought a house in the lower reaches of Hampstead. We spent our first night in it the day before we were due to leave for India, en famille, to visit my dying mother.

It was a symbolic night, that. For even as my mother lay in her death throes, cutting off the last links with the house in which I was born, for the first time in my adult life I was sleeping in a house which could conceivably become my new and permanent home.

Epilogue

'Friends and comrades, the light has gone out of our lives and there is darkness everywhere. I do not know what to tell you or how to say it ...' The cynical dissimulator was at it again of course, for these words were spoken by Jawaharlal Nehru immediately after Mahatma Gandhi's assassination. Though the voice intoned grief, the reality was that the last obstacle to his unquestioned supremacy had been fatefully and conveniently removed. He was now the undisputed head of an oligarchy; he had fulfilled an ambition he had nurtured since his Cambridge days, and which was till then thwarted only by the presence of the 'saint'. Hypocrisy is, to my mind, so endemic in the Indian character, and so often shored up by the liberal Left here, that these minor points need to be reiterated before a full-scale denunciation of current events can be launched.

I sound sour of course because there is no politesse in my nature. I have been called a TRAITOR in the Indian Parliament; I have been dubbed 'a writer of no consequence' in Indian newspapers. About the latter, my present readers must judge; about the former, I shriek a categorical 'No'.

Whatever the verdict, my sorrow and anger cannot be contained. Something I predicted long ago has come to pass, and it gives me no pleasure to say, 'I told you so'. A dynastic, authoritarian and despotic regime has been established in the land of my birth, and to quote Ouspensky, '...in spite of this, the process through which termites pass is called...evolution.'

I have no such fancy name for this latest adventure. It is no more indecent and vulgar for the Prime Minister of a vast country to refer personally to a writer in a foreign land* than for me to accuse her of ignorance, a species of cultural illiteracy, and that peculiar brand of Indian inferiority complex, which while accusing, manages totally to condemn itself.

But sorrow is basically what I feel. I went to India in August 1975

*'Why I had to clamp down', interview with Mrs. Gandhi by George Evans, *Sunday Telegraph*, 12th October, 1975.

for ten days and on my return to London published an article in the *Guardian* which they titled 'The Rape of the Lok',* where I described the nastiness of travelling around in India under present conditions.

Naturally I was apprehensively aware in advance that the Indian authorities might clamp me behind bars — it would not be the first time it had happened to a writer†. What I had not realized before going was the extent to which the day-to-day life of a people might be affected by a single decree, a mere stroke of the pen.

For even without going through the intricacies of the constitutional amendments recently rubber-stamped by the Indian Parliament under the dictates of the executive, it is clear that a concerted attempt has been made to convert the largest nation on the sub-continent into a police state. The result is the arbitrary exercise of dictatorial powers right down to the lowest levels, where no rationale is offered for actions, where the claims to freedom are flagrantly trampled on, and where elementary humanitarian demands are violated. People are held behind bars without trial, prisons are hideously overcrowded, torture has become the norm. Censorship effectively gags the writer; strikes are prohibited by law, and an atmosphere of intimidation and fear brings the petty tyrant uniquely into his own.

Of course those proverbial trains run on time, the *babus* turn up at work on the dot and a superficial aura of governmental efficiency is projected to the populace. But at what price, and for how long?

I had always lightly talked of democracy; I had made fun of Western liberal values. But it was only when these things were removed that I realized how unfunny and invaluable they were. In Delhi, for example, I could not raise my voice in a public place lest I be recognized. In Bombay old friends suddenly started making excuses so as to avoid being seen with me. I began to think of Warsaw, which I had once visited. And the simple fact of that comparison, even fleetingly in the mind, unnerved me.

Someone asked me where I lived. I had to tell him a lie, in order not to be found out; there was no sense in taking chances. On my flight down to Calcutta from Delhi, I travelled with the Minister of Information — a veritable Goebbels in disguise. What happened on my arrival at the airport was, of course, the classic leper reaction — no one wanted to be with me, in case I was spotted in their company. The Director of the TV centre in Calcutta, for instance, had been a close friend of mine for twenty years. When she saw me coming down from

---

*'Lok' in Hindi means the common people, as in 'Lok Sabha' (People's Assembly), which is the name of the lower house in the Indian Parliament.

†In August 1975 forty-one 'loyal' MPs tabled a motion in the lower house of the Indian Parliament demanding my extradition from Britain (in the mistaken belief that I still held an Indian passport) so that I could be tried for 'treason' in India.

the plane just behind her Minister, she scuttled clean out of view.

Of course one has to revise one's opinions; there are limits to which one can take the indulgence of Western liberal thought. But where at the end of the line does one stand, to what does one finally cling? A voice asks why condemn India where all freedom has been taken away from the common man, while you condone and even admire China? That voice has not heard a word called BETRAYAL. It is because of one's expectations, because of the lofty demands of idealism, that there is bitterness in the voice and iron in the soul.

Conceivably, this is good. Conceivably some people will benefit from the shock. But to convince me that this is being done for the good of the community and the common weal will require injections of high-power narcotics. It simply isn't true!

Politicians necessarily pervert theory — Disraeli did; de Gaulle ignored it. But the self-seeking, deliberate distortion of political philosophy which claims that it is acting constitutionally while it performs under the dictates of a mean-minded and powerful personality leads inevitably to moral deliquescence. While one can be professorially wise after the event, the fact of a gun at the back of your neck at three in the morning is unlikely to produce a Wittgensteinian reaction.

The difference between fetters and freedom is simple: in one state you cannot move about, in the other you can. The savage irony is that 'freedom' is more down-pressed in India today than it ever was under the British. Also, its assertion seems to be more worrying and dangerous to the authorities.

One relapses under these conditions into rehearsing the old verities: 'Freedom is indivisible'; 'The price of Liberty is eternal vigilance'. In a contest between independence and the promise of a future prosperity under bondage, which side are you on?

Posed with that ineffable and devastating question, the masses did not stand by on the sidelines. They obediently dropped their votes into the ballot box. And it was almost unanimously declared that a sharp-nosed lady with leonine features should rule the Kingdom.

The twist in the tale is that it did *not* happen on 26th June, 1975, when the 'State of Emergency' was declared and all fundamental rights were withdrawn from the Indian population. The real licence to tyrannize and deceive was donated by the electorate in 1971 (in a general election) to a woman who had already trodden rough-shod over all the rules in the game, whose personal record was one of total defilement of democratic values, and whose shrieks of 'neither I nor my son is a crook' were equal in pitch to the protestations of Richard Nixon.

And yet with all this known, certainly among those who wrote in the press and spoke on the radio, and with whispers of Court decadence reaching down to the lowliest villager, the 'toiling masses of India' gave her the largest ever majority in the Indian Parliament. Thus was the tiger first given a taste of the red meat of total dominance, and those who cautioned restraint were derided in private and mocked in public.

But then when the animal refused to be petted into civility, when its snarls of pathological mania rang out loud into the quiescent night of Indian squalor, when its autocratic teeth bit deep into the body of India's democratic polity, then hands were thrown up in amazed horror. Protest was gagged in the throat by fear.

What happened on 26th June, 1975 was the inevitable and logical conclusion of a process which had begun way back in 1969, when false votes were cast to split the Party and declare 'a mere slip of a girl' (the words of the then Deputy Prime Minister) the leader of a new and so-called radical Congress. Time-servers abounded in her entourage; she was said (with approbation!) to be 'the only man in her Cabinet'. Several journalists, now in purdah or in jail in India, were then her ardent admirers. The Western press, almost to a 'man', supported her ostensibly 'correct' radical stance. A few voices, including my own and Rajinder Puri's (the cartoonist) were raised against the tumultuous roar of acclaim, but we were dismissed as being either innocently insane or in the pay of reactionary forces.

The destiny of a nation was thus surrendered to the whims of an individual; the fortunes of one family were equated with 'the greater good' of six hundred million people. Inexorably, the train went rolling down the hill of Devi. With the proclamation of the 'State of Emergency', democracy was impaled on the spike of a psychotic's fantasy. Hysteric denunciation of 'foreign agents' took the place of reasoned debate. The still small voice of conscience was silenced across the length and breadth of the land. The hope that had been born some twenty-eight years previously when two centuries of foreign domination came to an end at midnight was callously massacred. The sorrowing groans of ardent well-wishers were angrily and meanly ignored. Yet again the dream of creating a free and just society was betrayed, as hired hands and shameless acolytes sang paeons of praise to 'the new Redeemer'. While all the pipsqueaks kowtowed, and died happily ever after.

And now, I can't go back *home* any more.